your essential
guide to what's
hip & happening

Cool!

Hong Kong

Martin Liu

mc Marshall Cavendish
Editions

Author's Note

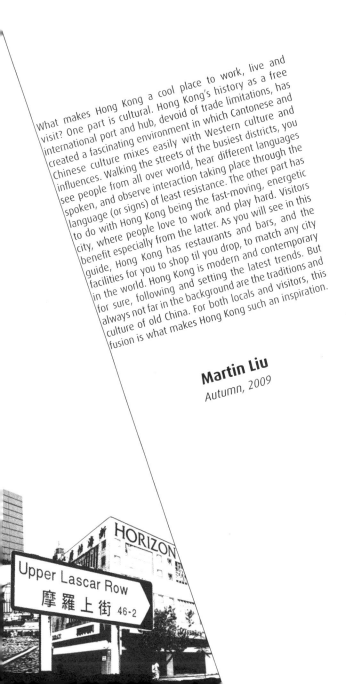

What makes Hong Kong a cool place to work, live and visit? One part is cultural. Hong Kong's history as a free international port and hub, devoid of trade limitations, has created a fascinating environment in which Cantonese and Chinese culture mixes easily with Western culture and influences. Walking the streets of the busiest districts, you see people from all over world, hear different languages spoken, and observe interaction taking place through the language (or signs) of least resistance. The other part has to do with Hong Kong being the fast-moving, energetic city, where people love to work and play hard. Visitors benefit especially from the latter. As you will see in this guide, Hong Kong has restaurants and bars, and the facilities for you to shop til you drop, to match any city in the world. Hong Kong is modern and contemporary for sure, following and setting the latest trends. But always not far in the background are the traditions and culture of old China. For both locals and visitors, this fusion is what makes Hong Kong such an inspiration.

Martin Liu
Autumn, 2009

HORIZON

Upper Lascar Row
摩羅上街 46-2

Relax

YOU'VE HAD A STRESSFUL PAST FEW WEEKS AND YOUR BODY AND MIND FEELS LIKE THEY HAVE BEEN PUT THROUGH A WRINGER. REJUVENATION AND REPAIR IS AT HAND IN THE WORLD-CLASS SPAS OF HONG KONG. YOU CAN EASILY SPEND THE BEST PART OF A DAY AT THESE VENUES; DON'T BE SURPRISED IF YOU COMPLETELY LOSE TRACK OF TIME. MOREOVER, IN THIS PART OF THE WORLD, MEN ARE FREQUENT VISITORS TO SPAS, AND MANY CATER SUPERBLY FOR THEM. SO, JUST RELAX...

The Oriental Spa

This 25,000-sq.ft spa occupies two floors and offers an amazing range of beauty and massage treatments and wellness facilities. The serene, indoor swimming pool, vitality pools, amethyst crystal steam rooms, Hamam steam and scrub room, herbal sauna, and the Roman laconium are the stand-out features. The spa is famous for its Time Rituals treatment, in which a therapist will sit with you to analyse your problems and concerns and then select a treatment programme for the day. The pilates and yoga studios offer courses which are very popular. For non-hotel guests, day passes can be bought. For couples after a treat, there is the luxury Sanctuary Suite equipped with amethyst crystal steam shower, vitality tub, futon mattress for relaxing and flat screen TV. The tranquil, temple-like interior was conceived by designer Peter Remedios and wellness architect Norbert Deckelmann, who have indeed created one of the great urban spas.

Landmark Mandarin Oriental, 15 Queen's Road, Central
Tel: 2132 0188 Website: www.mandarinoriental.com

Plateau

The Plateau was essentially Hong Kong's first luxury spa and set a benchmark for others over the recent years. One of its discernable features is the architecture, undertaken by John Morford (who was also responsible for the Park Hyatt Tokyo of *Lost in Translation* fame), with its beautifully thought-out angles and perspectives. Going to Plateau is rather like entering into a luxury boutique hotel. For the (three- or five-hour) treatment programmes, check in to one of the 14 rooms and suites, and then the spa comes to you. Each room has a king-sized futon where therapists apply their art. The décor is minimalist but enhanced by high-tech visual and audio equipment. The wet areas are beautifully designed with oversized baths and rain showers. The programmes are designed for pure indulgence and relaxation. Besides these, the Plateau has nine treatment rooms, where you can select from a broad menu of beauty and relaxation treatments. A popular option for men is the Plateau Massage (a combination of Shiatsu, Thai and Swedish techniques). The Carita Eye Treatment is popular with ladies. After all of this, go outside to the 50-metre pool (the largest outdoor pool in Hong Kong and heated during winter months) and take in the urban view.

Grand Hyatt Hong Kong, 1 Harbour Road
Tel: 2584 7688 Website: www.hyattpure.com

Bliss

If you have been to other Bliss spas in the US and UK, you will recognise the easy-going, fun nature of Bliss Hong Kong. A clever menu of services, together with rhythm and blues tunes, movie-while-you pedicure/ mancure and its now legendary brownie buffet, has quickly established Bliss as a popular alternative to the more traditional top-class offerings. *Time Out* rated it Hong Kong's best spa in 2008. True to its New York origins, the interior is dominated by a cyan-blue colour, which creates an aquatic and jazzy feel to the place. The Blissage 75 —a 75-minute head-to-toe massage—is one of the popular options. There are some interesting treatments that have a distinctive Asian twist, including the Ginger Rub, a scrub using ginger root, followed by a body wrap and full-body massage lasting 100 minutes. And being on the 73rd floor, ladies can have their nails polished and painted in the nail bar whilst enjoying an unforgettable view over the Kowloon Peninsula. Bliss is a slick and stylish venue, which has certainly livened up the Hong Kong spa scene in the short space of time it has been around.

W Hotel, 1 Austin Road West, Kowloon
Tel: 3717 2797 Website: www.blissworld.com

Spa

Spa at the Four Seasons offers 22,000 sq.ft of pure indulgence and pampering. Its arrival on the HK spa scene in 2005 certainly raised the already high standards a further notch. Helen Greene, director of Spa, describes the offering as "a fusion between state-of-the-art hydrotherapy facilities and Asian spirituality". When you arrive, do so early, because prior to your treatment you can enjoy the excellent facilities (Finnish sauna, amethyst crystal steam room, tropical steam showers, vitality pool, relaxation area with recliners, food and drinks) in the Vitality Lounge. When you are suitably prepared for your treatment, you are taken to one of the 16 marble rooms upstairs (if you can, get the one with the fantastic view of Victoria Harbour). The signature treatments are Asian inspired. The Pure Indulgence is a huge and award-winning favourite, using jojoba pearls, buttermilk, mango butter, honey, sweet orange oil and orange blossom water in a two-hour body massage and hair and scalp treatment. Other highlight treatments include the Oriental Jade Ritual (using jade stones to increase energy levels), the Aromatic Odyssey (deep, relaxing aroma massage) and the Oriental Infusion (balances *yin* and *yang* through the use of traditional herbs, Chinese infusions, elixir tonic and acupressure). Not surprisingly, clients leaving Spa do so with a distinct glow and step about them.

Four Seasons, 8 Finance Street, Central
Tel: 3196 8888 Website: www.fourseasons.com/hongkong

The Peninsula spa by ESPA

This spa is extremely well thought-out and designed from the point of view of facilities and experience. From the moment you enter the reception area, your senses begin to relax through the sounds of trickling water from the wall fountain and the soothing aromas emanating from aromatherapy oil burners. Dimmed lights, water themes and antique Chinese elements (the antique pine wood is reclaimed from original flooring from ancient Chinese houses) create an elegant and calming environment throughout.

A private elevator takes you up to the 9th-floor treatment rooms (14), relaxation areas and thermal suites. Guests are advised to arrive an hour in advance of their treatment to prepare their body and mind through the heating and cooling facilities (which include the Harbour-view sauna, crystal steam room, experience shower and crystal ice bath). Massage is the most popular treatment in any spa, and here, the Aromatherapy De-stressor Massage is the one to go for, lasting either 50 or 80 minutes, and consisting of a blend of massage techniques and comforting aromatic oils. Absolutely ideal if you have just got off the plane or escaped from a frantic week. The Peninsula Spa long established itself in the élite class and this, together with the Peninsula's legendary service, makes it one of Hong Kong's top pampering options.

The Peninsula, Salisbury Road, Tsim Sha Tsui, Kowloon
Tel: 2315 3322 Website: www.hongkong.peninsula.com

Architecture

HONG KONG WOULD NOT QUITE BE THE SAME WITHOUT THE EXTRAORDINARY SELECTION OF MODERN SKYSCRAPERS THAT ADORNS ITS SKYLINE. INDEED, HONG KONG'S LOVE FOR VERTICAL STRUCTURES EXTENDS TO SOME 7,680 SKYSCRAPERS, WHICH IS MORE THAN NEW YORK HAS. TAKING A STROLL ALONG THE HARBOUR IN TSIM SHA TSUI AND LOOKING ACROSS TO HONG KONG ISLAND PRESENTS AN ICONIC VIEW OF MODERN ASIAN ARCHITECTURE. AND THIS IS PROBABLY AS GOOD A START AS ANY IN YOUR TOUR OF HONG KONG'S GREAT ARCHITECTURAL STRUCTURES.

The Hong Kong Cultural Centre

The Hong Kong Cultural Centre, overlooking Victoria Harbour, has received mixed reactions. Purists view it as nothing more than a sports centre. Opened in 1989, it has had to work hard to win the affections of locals and visitors alike. Today, it functions beautifully as a venue for the arts. And some people are even beginning to appreciate the fine modern lines and architectural thought that went into creating the structure. Whatever people say about it, the Hong Kong Cultural Centre has become an iconic structure in Kowloon, with thousands flocking to it during major holidays.

10 Salisbury Road, Tsim Sha Tsui, Kowloon

Jardine House

Jardine House, 52 stories high, held the title of tallest building in Hong Kong during the 1970s, thus revealing its age in comparison to other structures today. But it became a benchmark for other architects and constructors as Hong Kong underwent further vertical modernisation thereafter. Jardine House's distinctive circular windows are in fact part of the architect's (Palmer and Turner) design to reduce the structure's weight, necessary due to the fact that it was built on what was then the most expensive reclaimed land in the world.

1 Connaught Place, Central

HSBC Building

The Hong Kong and Shanghai Bank (HSBC) Building has all the hallmarks of a Norman Foster design. Standing 179 metres high, its modern concept and obvious expression of technology and structure really did make people stop and stare when it first appeared in 1985. If you enter into the space directly below, you will be presented with a striking view of the inner workings of the building. Today, the HSBC Building is dwarfed somewhat by the other structures around it, but it continues to be one of Asia's leading architectural landmarks.

1 Queen's Road, Central

Bank of China Tower

People say the Bank of China Tower was built specifically to outshine its competitor, the HSBC Building. Its meat cleaver profile, facing the HSBC Building, certainly does not help to deflect that impression. Designed by IM Pei, it was opened in 1990, filled with symbolism in the run up to China reclaiming Hong Kong back from the British. It was no simple project building a 70-storey, 305-metre structure on steeply sloping land. But through its mirrored glazing, clean styling and diagonal motif, the Bank of China Tower has successfully emerged as a dominant feature in the Central skyline. There is a small public viewing gallery on the 43rd floor and also one of the 70th floor (this one by appointment only). One slightly negative fact about the building is that it has bad *feng shui*, which in this part of the world is considered not to be so good.

1 Garden Road, Central

Two IFC

Two IFC is the current big daddy of them all in Hong Kong, rising to 415 metres and containing 88 (to qualify as being very auspicious in Chinese culture) stories. It is located slightly away from the hub of Central, towards the Macau Ferry Terminal. As a result, its size is disproportionate to its immediate harbour-front neighbours, making it seem ever more impressive when viewed from Tsim Sha Tsui. Obelisk in shape, the structure was designed by Cesar Pelli and opened in 2003, and is now home to a luxury shopping mall and various major corporations occupying grade A offices. During the year of its opening, HSBC and Cathay Pacific put up an advertisement on the building's façade that covered 50 stories (an area of 19,000 metres squared), thus making it the largest ever advertisement put on a building.

8 Finance Street, Central

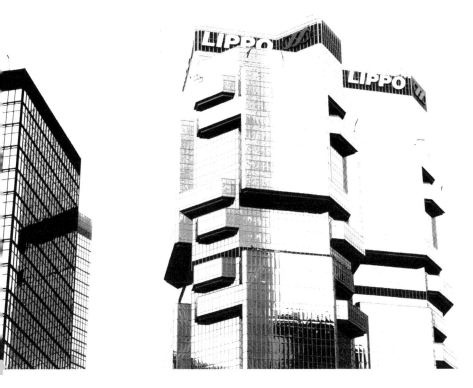

Lippo **Centre**

Moving east, the distinct shape and structure of the twin towers known today as the Lippo Centre rises out of Admiralty. Designed by American architect Paul Rudolph and opened in 1987, people often make out koalas climbing or clinging on to trees when looking at the Lippo Centre, hence its unofficial name of "The Koala Tree". Cubism and reflective glass play a big role in Rudolph's work, and the Lippo Centre is a culmination of this. Lippo Centre 1 stands at 172 metres; Lippo Centre 2 at 186 metres. Inside the main lobby, bas-relief murals from local artist Gerard d'Henderson create a dramatic interior setting.

89 Queensway, Admiralty

Highcliff

Further east is Highcliff, a remarkably thin, not to mention tall, all-residential structure in the shape of a double ellipse. If it weren't for Norman Foster's Gherkin in London, Highcliff (designed by Dennis Lau and Ng Chun Man) would have taken Gold instead of Silver in the prestigious Emporis Skyscraper Awards in 2004. Standing majestically on a south slope in Happy Valley, it is of course the highest residential building in Hong Kong and the 95th tallest building in the world, measuring 252 metres high (73 stories). Being so thin for such a tall building, a passive wind damper had to be fitted to the roof to protect the structure against Hong Kong's annual typhoons. Its modern design elegance and azure blue makes Highcliff quite a sight to behold.

41d Stubbs Road, Happy Valley

Tsing Ma **Bridge**

The journey to or from the airport will take in the Tsing Ma Bridge. A classic suspension bridge opened in 1997, it's the seventh longest of its kind in the world (spanning 1,377 metres), and links the islands of Tsing Yi and Ma Wan. It has two decks: the upper carries six lanes of road traffic; the lower has two tracks for rail (which in fact makes it the world's longest suspension bridge for rail). Remarkably, it only took the Anglo Japanese Construction Joint Venture five years to build, in which 49,000 tonnes of structural steel was used. One can marvel at the technology of this bridge. But on a fine clear day, against the backdrop of blue sea, the sight of the bridge is simply breathtaking and has become one of Hong Kong's outstanding landmarks.

Chep Lap Kok Airport

Opened in 1998, Chep Lap Kok Airport remains one of most impressive construction projects of the modern era. Clean, spacious, environmentally-friendly and generally filled with grey materials and surfaces, it's not difficult to guess that Norman Foster was the architect behind the airport. Built on a largely artificial island reclaimed from two islands (Chek Lap Kok and Lam Chau), it has added almost 1% to Hong Kong's surface area. One of the most noticeable features is the sheer height of the building, which when first introduced was a source of amazement for passengers inside, but which has since become a common feature in new airport designs around the world. You are probably most likely to have more time to look around during your departure, which is indeed a worthwhile use of your final hour in Hong Kong. Despite the array of retail and food outlets that is associated with any major airport, Chek Lap Kok Airport has managed to retain a splendid level of space and calm, very much unlike the rest of Hong Kong.

Cool!

Hong Kong

Dining

LIKE ITS SHOPPING OPTIONS, HONG KONG IS A HAVEN FOR THOSE WHO ENJOY DINING OUT. GO VIRTUALLY ANYWHERE, AND ALMOST ANYTIME, AND THERE IS A DINING ESTABLISHMENT OF SOME KIND WITHIN WALKING DISTANCE. THIS IS IN PART A REFLECTION OF THE LOCAL PEOPLE'S LOVE OF FOOD, THEIR GENERAL RELUCTANCE TO COOK AT HOME AND HONG KONG BEING ONE OF ASIA'S MOST VIBRANT PLACES TO LIVE AND VISIT. PEOPLE JUST LOVE GOING OUT IN THE EVENINGS! THE SELECTION OF RESTAURANTS HERE ONLY TOUCHES ON THE RANGE AND DEPTH OF HONG KONG'S CULINARY WORLD. YET CERTAINLY FOR VISITORS, EACH ONE OF THESE RESTAURANTS FEATURED HERE HAS SOMETHING UNIQUE ABOUT THEM, PROVIDES AN AMBIENCE CONDUCIVE TO RELAXED DINING, AND ENABLES YOU TO LOOK BACK WITH SOME SENSE OF WONDERMENT. BUT IF NONE OF THESE TAKE YOUR FANCY, ALMOST EVERYONE IN HONG KONG HAS THEIR FAVOURITE EATING PLACE. YOU WON'T HAVE ANY PROBLEMS GETTING DECENT RECOMMENDATIONS.

Located in the Bohemian Star Street area in Wanchai is Cinecitta. Spacious and modern, the restaurant offers Roman specialties and classic Italian dishes in an environment inspired by La Dolce Vita and other classic movies of the post-war boom period in Italy. Restaurant manager Stefano Bassanese ensures the restaurant adheres strictly to Italian food culture. Cinecitta has a large menu to select from. The artichoke salad with shave parmesan is a favourite with regulars. The bucatini with pork cheek, onion, chilli and tomato sauce and the spaghetti with pancetta, black pepper and egg yolk are very good. The veal saltimbocca with tomato gratin is a signature secondi of Cinecitta's. Mr Bassanese's knowledge of Italian wines is extraordinary, resulting in Cinecitta holding probably the best Italian wine collection in Hong Kong. The walk-in wine cellar, made of glass and a spectacular design feature of the restaurant, gives guests the opportunity to select their wine under the guidance of Mr Bassanese. During the evening, candlelight softens the atmosphere and there are movies by Fellini and Vittorio de Sica running silently on a large screen in the back. If you are on Hong Kong island and pining for something Italian, Cinecitta offers traditional dishes in a stylish environment away from the hustle and bustle of Central and Soho.

GF, Starcrest Building, 9 Star Street, Wanchai
Tel: 2529 0199 Website: www.elite-concept.com

Dong Lai Shun

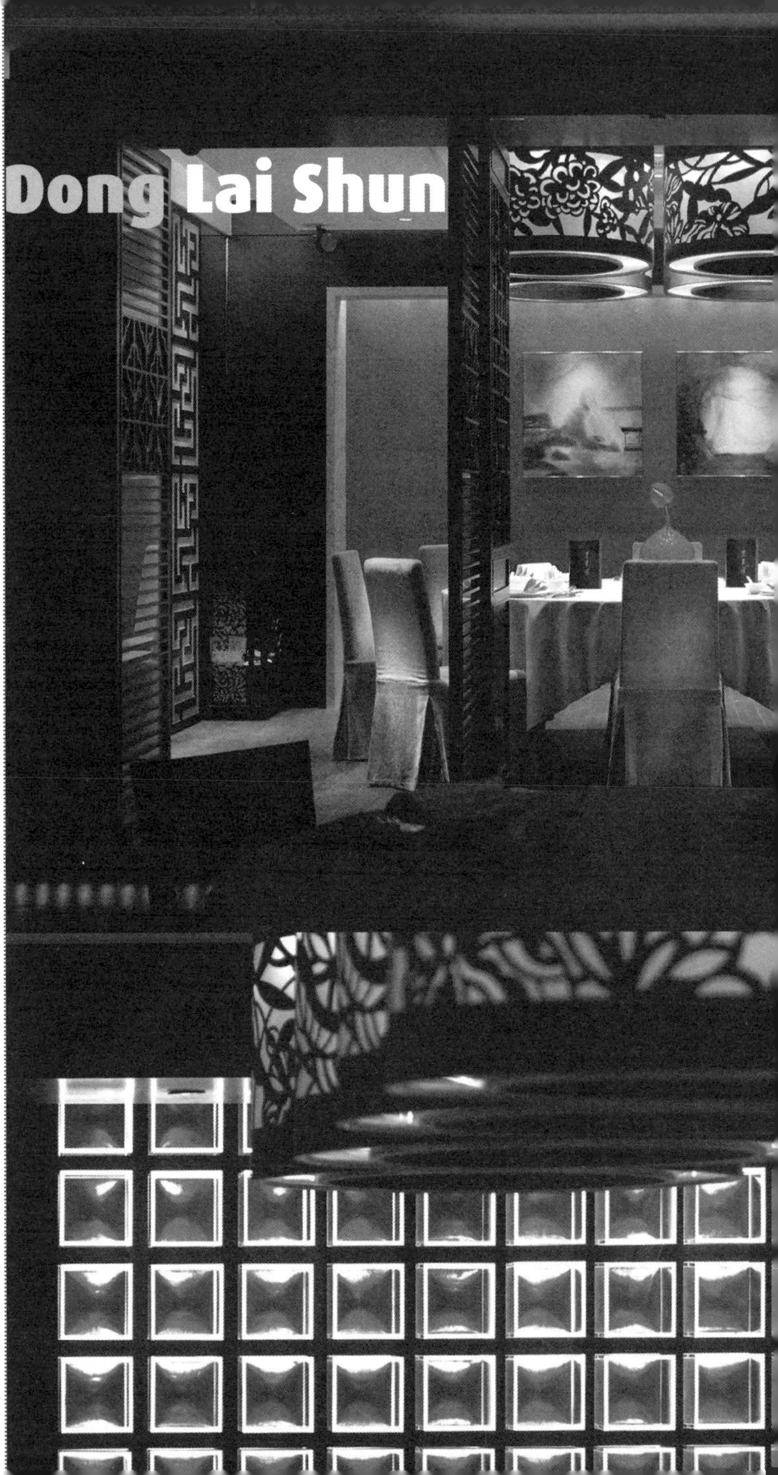

At Dong Lai Shun, renowned Hong Kong designer Steve Leung has created an elegant space that reflects a contemporary Beijing-style grand mansion. When you walk in, you will notice immediately the dark woods, Chinese antiques and spectacular grand lanterns based on southern Yangtze paper-cut folk art. Dong Lai Shun was founded over 100 years ago in Beijing and is known for its authentic Shuan Yang Rou dishes that consist of eight special ingredients. Dong Lai Shun in Hong Kong was opened in 2004 and has become a major player in the high-end Chinese cuisine scene. It offers a mix of Beijing and Huaiyang recipes (the latter, together with Cantonese, Shandong and Sichuan cuisines, make up the four Chinese gastronomic treasures). This is overseen by Kenny (Kwok Keung) Chan, one of Hong Kong's leading chefs of Beijing and Shanghainese dishes and a frequent visitor to those regions for new ingredients and ideas. Favourite appetizers with local diners are sautéed duck and smoked duck egg. Dong Lai Shun is particularly famous for its hand-sliced Mongolian mutton and seasonal crab dishes. And the dessert menu requires serious consideration (chilled chrysanthemum and pumpkin pudding is heavenly). If you are seeking a unique Chinese dining experience in Hong Kong, Dong Lai Shun should be on your list.

B2F, The Royal Garden Hotel,
69 Mody Road, Tsim Sha Tsui,
Kowloon
Tel: 2733 2020
Website: www.rghk.com

FINDS

FINDS (an acronym for Finland, Iceland, Norway, Denmark, Sweden) is one of the most popular nightspots in Lan Kwai Fong, but it also contains one of Hong Kong's best restaurants (*HK Tatler* 2009). Head chef Jaako Sorsa from Finland describes the dishes as "modern northern European cooking, with a strong Scandinavian influence". The dishes are presented in a modern fashion, but there is an honest and real taste to the food. Some of Jaako's favourite foods to cook are salmon (the house-smoked salmon filet is very popular and is smoked with wood imported from Finland), venison tenderloin and beef rydberg (a dish to share, but often you end up having it yourself). The set menus are creative and constantly evolving and there is also an all-night dining menu for partygoers. As well as maintaining FINDS' cutting edge, Jaako Sorsa is heavily involved in the training of Hong Kong's up-and-coming chefs as president of the Hong Kong chapter of the gastronomical association Disciples of Escoffier. The décor in FINDS is cool and sophisticated, inspired by winter in Scandinavia and the Nordic love for simplicity and open spaces. Hong Kong offers a huge variety of eating experiences, but FINDS definitely belongs to the category of "different" in terms of its dishes and décor.

2F, LKF Tower, 33 Wyndham Street, Central
Tel: 2522 9318 Website: www.finds.com.hk

cool!

Hong Kong

Zuma

If you want something Japanese in a sophisticated and vibrant atmosphere, Zuma in Central is a good bet. Those of you who have been to Zuma in London will be familiar with the touches and philosophy of co-founder Rainer Becker. Based on two floors, the lower level contains the main dining area and three dramatic open kitchens: the main kitchen, the sushi counter and the robata grill counter. Baby chicken marinated in barley miso and oven roasted on cedar wood is a signature dish. Miso-marinated black cod is another favourite. And the spicy beef tenderloin with sesame, sweet soy and red chilli is the must-try dish from the robata counter. This is contemporary

(as opposed to fusion) Japanese
food in which traditional Japanese
ingredients are used. Go up the
stunning spiral staircase for a very
comfortable bar and lounge area.
Here you will find one of Hong
Kong's finest collections of sakes,
with a resident sake *kikizakeshi*
on hand to serve premium sake
by the glass. If you don't fancy
sake on its own, there are some
quite spectacular cocktails (the
Rubabu—a rhubarb infused sake
shaken with Ketel One vodka and
fresh passion fruit—is so popular
that it often has to be suspended
until more rhubarb can be brought
in). Many of the dishes are ideal for
sharing for groups. And get there
a little early to enjoy a cocktail or
two before dining.

5&6F, The Landmark, 15 Queen's Road, Central
Tel: 3657 6388 Website: www.zumarestaurant.com

Ming Court

The Mongkok area is best known for its street food and night market, but recent modernisation and regeneration in the area has seen the creation of the Langham Place Hotel (see page 152), and within that, the Michelin-starred Ming Court restaurant. Ching Dynasty statues and Chinese landscape paintings form the basis of a stylish, curved interior. But look out of the windows, and you see an extraordinary urban picture of high rises and the wet market, a stark reminder of life on the streets. The menu is sophisticated, contemporary Cantonese. The deep-fried lobster with cheese has won awards and the simmered abalone with vinegar is another specialty of chef Tsang Chiu King. Ming Court is also highly recommended for its dim sum menu at decent prices. Shrimp dumplings, steamed custard buns with egg yolk, pan-fried buns with assorted mushrooms and original stir-fry dishes are the main delights. Exploring Mongkok is part of the Hong Kong experience. Lunch or dinner at the Ming Court provides an extra dimension to that.

6F, Langham Place Hotel, 555 Shanghai Street, Mongkok, Kowloon
Tel: 3552 3300 Website: www.hongkong.langhamplacehotels.com

Hutong

Sure, Hutong offers spectacular views of Victoria Harbour, but try not to let that distract you entirely from the excellent food (a Michelin-starred restaurant, 2009) and seductive interior. Designed in the style of the ancient courtyards of Beijing, the restaurant is a mix of old China within a dark, minimalist setting of elm wood and glass. Ornate carved wood screens and chairs, red silky lanterns and decorated bamboo bird cages add further to the visual experience. Executive chef Calvin Yeung's love of Chinese heritage and décor is combined with his enthusiasm for Northern Chinese cuisine. Hutong's signature dishes are crispy (de-boned) lamb ribs, bamboo clams steeped in Chinese rose wine and chilli padi, crispy soft shelled crab with Szechun red pepper, and scallops with fresh pomelo. They being traditional Northern Chinese, the dishes can be a touch on the spicy side. But don't be shy in asking your waiter for recommendations to suit your tastes. The visual experience of the interior is carried through to the dishes, which are served on Chinese porcelain and ceramic plates and carefully arranged to resemble pieces of art. The homemade coconut ice-cream provides a perfect ending to your evening's dining. It would be easy to forget that you are at the top of a modern skyscraper, if it weren't for the fantastic vista of the harbour, which has to have the last word in any write-up of Hutong.

28F, 1 Peking Road, Tsim Sha Tsui, Kowloon
Tel: 3428 8342 Website: www.aqua.com.hk

Caprice

For that special occasion, or if you are simply pining for the best possible French *haute* cuisine, look no further than Caprice. Rated as one of the top 10 restaurants outside of France, the team is headed by chef Vincent Thierry and house manager Jeremy Evrard, both previously with Cinq in Paris. It's difficult not to talk so enthusiastically about the cuisine here. Produce used in the kitchen is imported from France and the signature dishes are langoustine ravioli and challans duck filet. The nine-course "A Taste of Caprice", which changes four times a year according to the seasons,

is seriously worth considering. Monsieur Evrard describes the dishes as authentic French, that are light and refreshing, yet rich in taste and flavour. The wine list is equally spectacular: some 1,000 separate bins available from the great vineyards around the world. Monsieur Evrard has a great passion for cheese, which is delivered weekly from Alsace and kept in a specially built, humidity-controlled cellar. It's perhaps not so surprising to hear Jeremy also gives cheese and wine classes in his spare moments. Besides its dishes, Caprice offers elegant décor, a spacious lay out and spectacular views of Victoria Harbour and the Kowloon Peninsula. There is an open kitchen integrated into the design of the main dining area, which offers a fascinating show of chefs at work as well as a sensory experience from the delicious aromas circulating. A Michelin-starred restaurant? *Bien sûr*.

6F, Four Seasons Hotel, 8 Finance Street, Central
Tel: 3196 8860 Website: www.fourseasons.com

Lung King Heen

Is Lung King Heen really the best Chinese restaurant in the world? That debate started when the restaurant was awarded three Michelin stars (2009), the only restaurant in Hong Kong to receive such an accolade. Moreover, chef Chan Yan Tak is the only Chinese chef ever to have three stars pinned on him. The cuisine on offer is Cantonese, with an emphasis on seafood. The best Cantonese cuisine consists of fresh ingredients, clear flavours and contrasting textures. Lung King Heen certainly comes out very highly in that regard. There is a short but delightful *dim sum* list which forms a wonderful appetiser. The main courses should include a seafood dish of some kind, at which Chef Chan excels. The barbequed suckling pig is a favourite with Hong Kong visitors. The menu is extensive and ranges from relatively humble and well-known dishes (barbequed pork with honey) to more intricate ones (chicken baked in clay with black Perigord truffle). And don't miss out on the exquisite desserts. In fact, the latter is a hard choice to make, so go for the Lung King Heen dessert sampler. The waiting staff is really quite fantastic and knowledgeable, always willing and able to enhance your experience. With all the wonderful cuisine, there seems hardly the need to mention the undulating silver-leaf ceiling, and overall sleek and understated modernity of the restaurant interior. Lung King Heen means "view of the dragon", but the views of Victoria Harbour are subtle and certainly not demanding of your attention, which makes a nice change. So, is it the best Chinese restaurant in the world? Well, if it is not, then it comes pretty damn close!

4F, Four Seasons Hotel, 8 Finance Street, Central
Tel: 3196 8860 Website: www.fourseasons.com

Azure

Azure, located on the 29th and 30th floors of the Hotel LKF (see page 156), offers top notch ambiance and spectacular views. Some would say it's a lounge bar, others see it as a restaurant. You can go and enjoy both quite effortlessly. Cleverly designed by Andre Fu, the casual bar is located on the 29th floor and has a lively buzz about it after work. The woody library interior is filled with velvet couches, lacquered low tables, and various unique artifacts, which does make spending time here an easy option. And being a real bar, there is a pool table to bring out the competitive spirit in you. Go up the winding staircase, and you enter the tall-ceilinged restaurant, decorated in cool blue colours. Here, the views of the city are simply amazing, and provide a wonderful accompaniment to any special evening dinner. Dutch-Canadian chef Peter Bakker offers contemporary cuisine, with a firm emphasis on getting the flavour and texture right. Lobster fettucine is the most popular dish amongst regulars, but the Kurobuta pork rack is not far off. One of Bakker's favourites is Thai black cod, which is poached in coconut milk and infused with Thai flavours and which certainly tempts your taste buds. Making a reservation is highly recommended. Moreover, if you want a certain amount of peace and quiet whilst dining, make sure you don't dine too late. By about 10.30pm, the DJ starts his set and a party atmosphere ensues, with increasing numbers of people coming up to the 30th floor and heading out to the outdoor terrace (which has become one of Hong Kong's hottest spots to see and be seen). The food, the views, the atmosphere—Azure seems to have it all.

29F, Hotel LKF, 33 Wyndham Street
Tel: 3518 9330 Website: www.azure.hk

Amber

As you enter the dining room at Amber, it's hard not to stop and gaze at the remarkable ceiling sculpture conceived by designer Adam Tihany. Consisting of 4,320 brass tubes, the sculpture hangs like a grandiose pipe organ, impressing all beneath it. Fortunately, executive chef Richard Ekkebus is able to take your mind off the ceiling with an innovative and ambitious menu. Essentially French, there is a contemporary, light feel to Ekkebus' cooking, with a strong emphasis on using the finest and freshest ingredients from around the world. Dungeness crab in five textures and

four temperatures, langoustine with Iberian pork belly, and Tasmanian salmon with kyuri cucumber are prepared and presented with great style and care, and are quite rightly deemed signature dishes. Amber has a chocolate *sommelier* on board, and thus, excels with desserts (the crisp hazelnut and caraibe chocolate bar served with moccachino is delightful). Being in the heart of Central, business types tend to take over during lunchtimes (and what a place it is for those extended power lunches). But during the evenings, Amber provides a relaxed and stylish environment to enjoy French *haute* cuisine of the Michelin 2-star variety (2009).

The Landmark Mandarin Oriental, 15 Queen's Road, Central
Tel: 2132 0066 Website: www.mandarinoriental.com

Ye Shanghai

Lovers of Shanghainese cuisine rate this chic establishment very highly. The setting and mood is 1930s Shanghai (dark woods, subdued lighting, hanging lanterns) with some subtle contemporary features. Excellent for groups of diners, the alcoves nevertheless offer a certain amount of privacy for twin diners. The food is authentically Shanghainese, but the menu also features dishes from the neighbouring provinces of Zhejiang and Jiangsu. The signature dishes are steamed pork dumplings, sea cucumber with mild chilli sauce, baked stuffed crab shells, and sautéed minced chicken with pine nuts served with sesame pastry pockets. For dessert, the Shanghai deep-fried eggwhite stuffed with banana and red-bean paste or the black sesame ice cream are absolutely delicious and firm favourites with regulars. The amount of choice can be somewhat overwhelming, but the set menu is very reliable. Or simply ask the attentive but not over-bearing waiting staff for guidance. "Ye Shanghai" means "Shanghai Nights" and this is indeed an establishment for evening dining. And for that, it is stylish, comfortable and unpretentious.

6F, Marco Polo Hotel, Harbour City, Canton Road, Tsim Sha Tsui, Kowloon
Tel: 2376 3322 Website: www.elite-concepts.com

Kitchen

If you are seeking comfort food, Kitchen has much to offer. Overseen by Kiwi chef Michael Poutawa, the restaurant is beginning to generate real buzz locally and seems equally popular during lunch and evening times. Being part of W Hotel (see page 164), it's no surprise Kitchen has an urban and hip feel about it. There's a lively food preparation area which features a spacious communal table (a great option for single dining), surrounded by interesting artworks and cuisine books. The other part of the restaurant contains expansive and spectacular bay windows that offer views of the Western Harbour. You will probably be familiar with most of the dishes on the menu: steaks, fish, chicken, burgers (try the Spa Burger), salads... essentially, home foods, with an Asian and contemporary touch, and in the main created with organic ingredients. If you are feeling a little indecisive, during the evening, there is an excellent buffet presentation in which you can select four main dishes. And the Sunday brunch is rapidly becoming legendary in Hong Kong (perhaps the free-flowing champagne and oysters has something to do with that).

W Hotel, 1 Austin Road West, Kowloon Station, Kowloon
Tel: 3717 2222 Website: www.whotels.com/hongkong

Yun Fu

Yun Fu is a relative newcomer to the restaurant scene in Hong Kong having opened in mid-2007. But for those in the know, it is highly regarded. Part of Yun Fu's fame comes from its mystical and discreet tone. Entering through heavy, ornate oak doors, you descend a steep, budha-lined staircase, accompanied by slightly eerie music, into a dungeon-like, subterranean space. You are greeted first by an extraordinary circular bar area with walls made of stone. Yun Fu is the latest project from Aqua Restaurant Group's Calvin Yeung (see also Hutong, page 48): "The interior design is characterised by the theme of a 'circle' which, in Chinese tradition, signifies 'unity' and 'infinity'". The bar's signature cocktails are based on traditional Chinese wines and liquor. Scenes from vintage Chinese martial arts movies are projected onto a curved wall. A hallway, flanked by old Chinese wood and glass doors, takes you through to the main dining room and private rooms. Red lanterns, antique furniture and Hadda silks are very noticeable and create a sultry atmosphere to dine in. Yun Fu's menu offers gourmet Chinese dishes from diverse regions (including Shanghai, Beijing and Tibet). The favourites include succulent roasted whole duck marinated in Chinese tea leaves and herbs, wok-fried fish filet with golden salted egg yolk, and marinated lamb ribs roasted with herbs. After dinner, return to the bar, where live DJ music creates a chilled atmosphere to round off the night.

BF, 43-45 Wyndham Street, Central
Tel: 2116 8855 Website: www.aqua.com.hk

China Tee **Club**

The China Tee Club is an oasis of an establishment for lunch or afternoon tea after a hard few hours of shopping in Central. The Pedder Building itself is one of the few buildings of 1930s Hong Kong remaining. Inside, the sweeping ceiling fans and traditional Malaysian interior provides a calm colonial feel. Technically, this is a members-based club. But daily memberships for visitors are available for a small fee (phone ahead). The lunch menu is Southeast Asian (with the Hainan chicken rice a firm favourite) and Western (with a touch of Eastern influence). At tea time, English tea sets are served as well as steamed Chinese dumplings and other popular *dim sum* dishes in bamboo baskets. If you are on your own, get a table by the window, which offers an addictive view over the bustle of Peddar Street.

1F, Pedder Building, 12 Pedder Street, Central
Tel: 2521 0233 Website: www.chinateeclub.com.hk

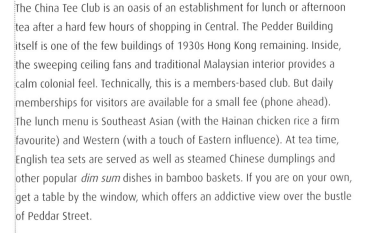

Lobby at Peninsula

Afternoon tea at the Peninsula is a somewhat predictable thing to do when visiting Hong Kong, and as a result, you might find yourself lining up in a touristy queue (assuming you are not a hotel guest). Nevertheless, there is something quite magical about taking tea in this establishment, which continues to be thought of very fondly by locals and not just visitors. The elegant three-tier afternoon tea set together with Peninsula tea blends is the obvious choice. The bottom tier contains scones made from a recipe unchanged for half a century. The centre plate contains savouries such as finger sandwiches (crust removed) and mini quiches. And the top tier holds cakes and pastries. In short, a very English offering. But if you want something different, lobby manager Peter Tang recommends hot chocolate and a Suzie Q sandwich (chargrilled beef, baked with mozzarella in a soft bun). All of this is accompanied by marble-topped tables, Tiffany & Co chinaware, live classical music and undeniably comfortable chairs. The Lobby has retained its original structure, décor and fittings, providing an example of what grand buildings were like in 1920s Hong Kong. During the 1950s, unmarried ladies sat on the east side, whilst married ones occupied the west side. Today, regulars sit at their favourite tables and have been doing so for years.

The Peninsula, Salisbury Avenue, Tsim Sha Tsui, Kowloon
Tel: 2315 3171 Website: www.hongkong.peninsula.com

Life Cafe

Located opposite to the Mid-Levels escalator, Life Café offers organic vegetarian and vegan food and drinks, based on a very sound eco-friendly approach. There is a welcoming deli counter on the ground floor with colourful salads and a constantly changing menu. Vegetable lasagna and tofu, vegetable samosas, and various pasta dishes are some of the firm favourites. The diversity of drinks is equally impressive, ranging from protein shakes, juices and tea to organic wines and beers. On the floor above is a relaxing restaurant environment, and further up is a fantastic open-air, wooden-decked roof which is perfect for lunch or drinks. Everyone is relaxed, friendly and laid back—and most likely very healthy—which is exactly what you would expect in a place like Life Café.

10 Shelley Street, (bet. Hollywood Road & Staunton Street), Soho
Tel: 2810 9777 Website: www.lifecafe.com.hk

DIM SUM

If you are in Hong Kong, you simply must have *dim sum* at least once. Locals and regular visitors will have their own favourite restaurants, such is *dim sum* a daily part of life here. Essentially, the choice is vast, but here are a few to get you started.

Luk Yu **Tea House**

The most famous of the old-style teahouses is Luk Yu Tea House. Black ceiling fans, wood paneling, marble tabletops and even brass spittoons are some of the traditional charateristics of Luk Yu which has been operating here since 1933. Reservations for the revered first floor is nearly impossible to get, because it is (unofficially) reserved for regulars.

24-26 Stanley Street, Central
Tel 2523 1970

Yung Kee

Yung Kee is another old-timer, opening in 1942, when it sold roast goose. Today, it is still renowned for its roast goose and other Cantonese style roast meats. *Dim sum*, however, has its place with some of Hong Kong's finest *dim sum* chefs working here.

32-40 Wellington Street, Central
Tel: 2522 1624

Tsui Hang Village

Tsui Hang Village is named after the home village of Dr Sun Yat-Sen. The interior is traditional Chinese with waiters and waitresses decked out in old-style costumes. Be prepared to wait for a table during late mornings and lunchtimes at this very popular establishment.

2F, New World Tower, 16-18 Queens Road, Central
Tel: 2524 2012

翠亨邨

TSUI HANG VILLAGE RESTAURANT

Maxims

The Maxims restaurant in City Hall, recently renovated, provides visitors with experience of a big *dim sum* restaurant, with all the noise, clatter (of carts delivering *dim sum*) and people that goes with that. Because City Hall is a popular marriage registry, expect wedding parties as well.

2F, City Hall, Central
Tel: 25378607

Grand **Stage**

At the Grand Stage restaurant, inside the colonial styled Western Market building, you can enjoy daily tea dance performances while having your *dim sum*. The interior is one of the joys of this location.

Western Market, Des Voeux Road, Sheung Wan
Tel: 2815 2311

Dragon-I

Cool!

Hong Kong

For a more modern and hip approach to *dim sum* dining, go to Dragon-I, which at night is one of Hong Kong's coolest nightspots (see page 136). Take one of the outdoor tables, listen to the birds chirping, and go for the "all you can eat" *dim sum* option for about HK$150.

UGF, 60 Wyndham Street, Central
Tel: 3110 1222
Website: dragon-i.com.hk

NOODLES

Besides *dim sum*, Hong Kong's other perennial favourite is noodles of all kinds. Wherever you are, you won't have to go far to find a noodle shop. Noodles are eaten for breakfast, lunch, dinner or just as a snack

Mak's

Mak's is just like virtually any noodle shop in Hong Kong. It's busy, hot and more often than not, you end up sharing a tiny table with strangers. But the *wanton* noodles in soup is truly fantastic. Plus, it is frequented by a few Hong Kong movie stars, which perhaps puts Mak's slightly ahead of its many competitors. Movie star or not, you don't loiter in these noodle shops. Once you have finished your food, it's time to go, so the next customer can grab your seat.

77 Wellington Street, Central
Tel: 2854 3810

Miso Cool

For slightly alternative Japanese ramen noodles and other Japanese fast dishes, try Miso Cool. At lunch time, expect queues for the lift that snakes out on to Stanley Street. Inside you will find a colourful and lively interior, with rock/alternative music (selected from a giant ipod-like duke box on the wall) blasting out to add to the atmosphere. Be warned, this is not a place for a quiet, cosy chat! The pork ramen is king here, but if you want to try something different, the beef ramen with tomato soup is surprisingly good. The baked oysters and deep fried soft-shelled crab are also popular dishes. For a refreshing drink, try the grape kyoko smoothie. The menu is essentially Japanese with a modern and quirky twist. Also, both noodle and rice dishes are on the large size. For about HK$50, it's no wonder this place has become an instant hit. Miso Cool is another project of Gilbert Yeung (of Dragon-i fame). So there is inevitably a hip feel about the place, which also helps to attract the crowds.

1F, Stanley 11, No.11 Stanley Street, Central
Tel: 2868 3738

Shopping

"WHAT IS THERE TO DO IN HONG KONG BESIDES SHOPPING AND EATING?" THAT MIGHT BE A RATHER SIMPLISTIC WAY OF SUMMING UP THE DELIGHTS OF HONG KONG. BUT WHEN IT COMES TO SHOPPING, NO ONE IN THEIR RIGHT MIND COULD DENY HONG KONG HAS IT ALL. MAINSTREAM SHOPPERS HEAD STRAIGHT FOR THE MALLS, WHICH ARE QUITE SIMPLY SUPERB. FOR THE SLIGHTLY MORE ADVENTUROUS, THERE ARE THE MANY INDIVIDUAL STORES WHICH HAVE SPRUNG UP, HELD FIRM AND ACHIEVED STATUS WITHIN THE FASHION AND LIFESTYLE COMMUNITY. EVEN MORE ADVENTUROUS SHOPPING COMES IN THE FORM OF OUTDOOR MARKETS, MINI MALLS AND OUTLET MALLS. SO, YES, SHOPPING WILL MOST LIKELY TAKE A FAIR CHUNK OUT OF YOUR TIME SPENT IN HONG KONG. BUT THERE'S ADVENTURE, DISCOVERY, NOT TO MENTION BARGAINS, TO BE HAD HERE!

SHOPPING MALLS

On the list that defines what Hong Kong is exceptionally good at, luxury shopping malls must rank fairly high. During weekends, they act as hubs of activity for many locals, providing air-conditioned environs to shop, eat and drink. Visitors to Hong Kong eventually end up in at least one of them. There are the old favourites like Landmark (14 Des Voeux Road, Central), Pacific Place (88 Queensway, Admiralty) Times Square (Causeway Bay) and Harbour City (3-27 Canton Road, Tsim Sha Tsui, Kowloon). You can't go too far wrong with any one of these. But for something more recent, try the following, which have cemented Hong Kong's status as a shopping mecca.

IFC Mall

The IFC Mall is next to Hong Kong's tallest building, Two IFC. With 200 shops containing mainly high-end brands set over three levels, the IFC Mall has become Hong Kong's preeminent shopping destination. This is a world of contemporary, curving shapes and an atmosphere that borders on sterility, but which nevertheless has proved to be a magnet for the hip, well-heeled shopper. The mall is anchored by Lane Crawford's flagship store, which covers 80,000 sq.ft, with a distinctive interior created by design house Yabu Pushelberg that is a fusion of fashion, art and architecture. Various pieces of modern art are on display in the store, including sculptures by Hirotoshi

SHOE GAZING

ONE PERSON'S ANATHEMA IS ANOTHER PERSON'S DELIGHT AND AMONGST THE FASHION ELITE, THE LATTER IS OFTEN A VERTIGINOUS STACKED HEEL. SUPERFLUOUS BUCKLES, STUDS, AND EMBELLISHMENT ONLY SWEETEN THE DEAL. BECAUSE THE FASHION EDITOR IS A RARE BREED OF WOMAN WHO NOT ONLY WELCOMES THE PERIL OF A TOWERING PAIR OF STILETTOS, BUT RELISHES IT. HER INFLAMED, LACED FEET SERVING AS A BADGE OF HONOUR. LIKEWISE, A SLIP HERE OR THERE, A LINGER, A SIGN OF POOR TECHNIQUE RATHER INCISIVE SELECTION. AS IT SAYS YOU LOVE FASHION — THESE SCUFFED AND STACKED FLOOR-GRAZING MASTERPIECES SAY YOU'LL DIE FOR IT.

Sawada and Dennis Lin. Other notable features is the one-stop shop for Agnes b, called "agnes b. LA LOGGIA", which covers 15,000 sq.ft and is indeed a marvellous sight for Agnes b. devotees. As well as fashion, the location contains Fleuriste (florist), La Maison sur L'eau (travel concept store), Le Pain Grille (restaurant) and Delices (chocolate boutique). The cooler, hipper brand shops are found generally on the top floor, including the so-called "denim zone" which bunches together designer denim brands 7 For All Mankind, Evisu, True Religion and Lucky Brand Jeans. The IFC Mall also contains the world's third Puma Black store (after New York and Tokyo) which fuses sport with fashion, based on collaborations with leading fashion designers such as Alexander McQueen, Sergio Rossi and Schedoni. The ground floor is where you will find a range of beauty and cosmetics shops. And if you want to take an escapist break from all the shops, or need a destination to meet back at in 2–3 hours, the IFC Mall houses an excellent five-screen cinema which has the reputation of being the most comfortable in Hong Kong.

8 Finance Street, Central

Elements

Hong Kong's newest shopping centre is Elements, which resides in West Kowloon by the harbour. Designed by Benov (the architectural firm that created Bluewater in the UK, Europe's largest mall), Elements offers over 1 million sq.ft. of retail space, set over four levels, and is a prime example of contemporary Asian, perfectly formed, upscale shopping mall. The mall's plan is based on the Chinese *feng shui* principle of the five elements of nature—fire, water, earth, metal and wood—with each zone featuring a certain mix of retailers as well as various works of art (some interactive) reflecting the theme. For example, the Wood zone features health and beauty boutiques; the Earth zone contains high-street fashion; and the Metal zone contains luxury brands. Besides the attractions of shopping, there is a 12-screen cinema and ice-rink (in the Fire zone), as well as a large (700,000 sq.ft.) rooftop garden with several options for alfresco wining and dining. You can find all the usual mid–high end brands in Elements. But some of the features include Bals Tokyo (electic home

furnishings and accessories from Japan), Jimmy Choo (definitely for the
well-heeled), Onitsuka Tiger (cult sneakers), Kura Chika (carries the Porter
and Luggage Label range of bags designed and made in Japan by Yoshida
& Co), Anteprima Wirebag (contrarian, futuristic handbags), Ascot Chang
(one of Hong Kong's favourite tailors), and EQ:IQ (offers ready-to-wear
fashion and accessories that blends East and West). Because it is situated
on top of Kowloon train station (where you can check in and catch the
Airport Express), Elements offers a pleasant option to kill time before
heading off to the airport.

1 Austin Road West, Tsim Sha Tsui, Kowloon

Lee Gardens

If you can't quite handle the size and range of the mega-malls of Hong Kong, but still need to get to a mall laden with the great and mighty brands, then Lee Gardens offers a decent alternative. Located on the slightly more stylish side of Causeway Bay, there is a certain discreetness about Lee Gardens. Those in the know, for example, go to the Chanel store here because it offers the widest range of Chanel items in Hong Kong. The mall consists of two sites—Lee Gardens One and Two. Lee Gardens One contains the majority of the high-end brands. Gucci, Louis Vuitton, Ralph Lauren, Dior, Jean-Paul Gaultier, Hermès, as well as contemporary trendsetters such as Paul Smith, Y's Yohji Yamamoto, Anya Hindmarch, Zeta, and Anteprima are established here. This is not the mall for new or up-and-coming brands. Even during the weekend, the mall can seem quiet and blissful. There is a general culture of impeccable service, starting from the concierge desk, all the way through to the retailers and the food and beverage points. Lee Gardens has become a favourite with local celebrities, who are often seen wondering around. Certainly, these are the types who don't need crowds on their day off.

33 Hysan Avenue, Causeway Bay

Located in Causeway Bay along Kingston Street, Cleveland Street and running into Paterson Road, Fashion Walk is principally made up of ground-level, individual stores, adjoined to each other. Leaving one store, walking along the pavement outdoors into another, can be quite a refreshing experience after all those indoor malls. The fashion on offer here is mid-brandish, more cutting edge and urban. There are the regulars such as Adidas, Diesel, Guess, Calvin Klein, IT and Max Mara. But Causeway Bay today is considered to be the fashion district of Hong Kong, and even Fashion Walk pays homage to that. 5cm, Cabane de Zucca, Gomme, Juice, Dusty, GDS Lab, A.T, Chapel are some of the edgier stores here. It's not quite like power-shopping in the IFC, but strolling around Fashion Walk in the cooler evening air can make for a rather pleasant shopping experience.

Causeway Bay

JILL STUART

agnès b.
le pain grillé

KINGSTON STREET
PATERSON STREET

I.T

JILL STU

MINI MALLS

Due to Hong Kong's exorbitant rents and general scarcity
of land, especially in main retail locations, mini-malls (or
micro boutiques) have become an important feature on the
Hong Kong fashion and shopping landscape. These mini-
malls are found in buildings that were previously large
restaurants, banquet halls or cinemas. Located on several
floors, they consist of micro shops often in spaces the size
of a walk-in closet. They are accessible to young designers
and entrepreneurs due to the relatively low rents. Indeed,
many local fashion designers cut their teeth in such an
environment, and retail entrepreneurs import unusual and
experimental items from overseas (especially from Japan).
As a result, visitors and locals get to experience some of the
most cutting-edge and original designs in the Hong Kong
fashion scene as well new styles and ideas from abroad.

Rise Commercial Building

Three of the more interesting mini-malls are found in Causeway Bay and Tsim Sha Tsui. Rise Commercial Building is recognised as the pioneer of the mini-mall movement in Hong Kong. Opened in the late 1990s, it contains several floors of locally designed fashion and imports from Japan. Busy and popular, the vast majority of the micro boutiques appeal to the young and hip. Also, being more established, many retailers are not complete beginners, and have other retail ventures on the go. So expect varying opening hours, although in general the opening times are from late afternoon to 11 pm.

5-11 Granville Circuit, Tsim Sha Tsui, Kowloon

GI Mall

Also in Tsim Sha Tsui, not far from Rise, is GI Mall (GI being short for Granville Identity). Opened by local actor and director Stephen Chow Sing-chi, GI Mall has a greater commercial presence, with its ground floor entrance on one of Kowloon's busiest streets and a more open-plan (department store) approach to retailing. Like Rise, it appeals to the young and hip, but goes beyond fashion, with micro stores offering gadgets, stationery and other small and quirky items. In the streets linking Rise and GI can be found several independent fashion stores, which are well worth browsing.

34 Granville Road, Tsim Sha Tsui, Kowloon

Island Beverley

And in Causeway Bay resides Island Beverley, a four-floor mini-mall, crammed with some 160 boutiques, and known to virtually every local female with an interest in fashion. Certain designers here have regular customers and have been so successful that they even have seasonal catalogues. There are also a wide range of costume jewellery and accessories shops. Besides creativity and originality of products, there is tremendous diversity in these mini-malls.

1 Great St George Street, Causeway Bay

On Lan Street

What was once a dead-end street is now home to a row of high-end, trendsetting fashion boutiques. On Lan Street in Central consists of old townhouse buildings (dating back to the early 1900s), four stories high, most of which are made of stone, and are becoming increasingly rare in Hong Kong. Here you will find the flagship stores for Comme des Garçons, Martin Margiela, Mihara Yasuhiro, Ice Cream/Billionaire Boys Club, Hoods Permanence, and Ann Demeulemeester. Besides these, there are also Uma Miy (bags, shoes and accessories) and the edgy, high-end select store D-mop. For a quiet narrow street, On Lan serves up one hell of a boutique fest! And around the

corner, at 18 Wyndham Street, you will find F.I.L, which carries the iconic Japanese fashion brand Visvim, renowned for being supercool, not to mention super-stringent in its quality checking of each garment. To get a sense of what these old town houses were originally like, go into Maison Martin Margiela. The interior of the shop is mainly white, which enables you to get a good sense of the original structure. Oh, and the clothes look stunning in the minimalist environment as well. These distinct, individual stores certainly offer an above-average shopping experience, which puts On Lan Street on Hong Kong's quality shopping map.

Temple Street

When it comes to shopping, Temple Street Night Market (Kowloon—take the MTR to Jordan and head west for a few blocks on Jordan Road until you hit Temple Street) is undoubtedly a mass-tourist destination. But even the most discerning visitor cannot deny the market has its peculiar charm and atmosphere. So why not? Along a tight central corridor, with some 400 stalls either side, the merchandise consists of gadgets, souvenirs, toys and action figures, clothing, art pieces, cheap watches, luxury brand rip-offs and so on. In an area in the middle of the market,

you will find open-air food stalls (which are always packed) and an array of fortune tellers and face-readers who sit at tiny tables offering their predictions. Amongst aficionados and local DJs of hip hop, soul and dance music, Hip Hop (179A Temple Street) is a favourite destination, offering probably the best selection of such CDs in Hong Kong. Also, if you are looking for sneakers, go to Fa Yuen Street in Mongkok, not far from Temple Street, which is a haven for anyone who has a predilection for them. The stores Chicago and New York (on Nelson Street, just off Fa Yuen Street) sell high-end sneakers. Even when it is a hot steamy night, with hundreds of people milling around in the same tight spot, Temple Street Night Market remains one of Hong Kong's classic 8–11 pm night haunts.

Horizon Plaza

Outlet shopping is serious business in Hong Kong amongst its army of brand lovers. Horizon Plaza (Lee Wing Street, Ap Lei Chau) is the place to go for this less advertised but nevertheless instrumental form of designer shopping. Ap Lei Chau is slightly off the beaten track, located on the south coast of Hong Kong, and to get there, you can take a bus from Central (590M, 590A, 90B to Ap Lei Chau Estate Bus Terminal, followed by a shuttle to Horizon Plaza). Unless you are flat broke (through shopping downtown!), you are frankly better off taking a taxi (most taxi drivers will know "Horizon Plaza, at Ap Lei Chau"—you will recognise the building because it is, ironically, next to a Ferrari car showroom). The building itself is tall and non-descript, but inside you will find the outlet branches of Joyce Warehouse, Lane Crawford, IT, Armani, Club Monaco, Juicy Couture, Max Mara, Space (which includes Prada, Miu Miu and Helmut Lang), Bluebell (which includes Paul Smith and Moschino) amongst others. Everything is well organised and displayed, the range of sizes is reasonable, and there are indeed some incredible bargains to be had amongst the samples, factory-seconds and previous-season items. Lane Crawford provides the opportunity to stock up with basic, season-insensitive work clothes and additions from leading designers. There are decent cafes in the building and, besides fashion, other stores selling furniture, home accessories, gifts, toys and baby accessories. There are no awards for interior design here, but visitors don't seem to mind given their focus is firmly fixed on the price tags.

Lee Wing Street, Ap Lei Chau

Stanley Market

Stanley has undergone extensive modernisation over the past few years, but Stanley Market itself has remained more or less the same. Located in the southeastern side of Hong Kong Island, this waterfront promenade is familiar to every taxi driver. Come in the morning, have a late breakfast at one of the waterfront cafes on Main Street, and then head into the market. It's cramped and the ground is a little uneven in places, but regular visitors swear by the bed sheets and linens from Tong's (55 Main Street, Stanley, Tel: 2813 0337), which is indeed one of the market's most frequented stores. For those wishing to stock up on cashmere for the winter, stop at Fook Tak Ho (40A Main Street, Stanley, Tel: 2813 2002). Nothing spectacular, but there is a broad range of colours to choose from at sensible prices. Ladies seeking a silk *cheongsam* to take home with them should visit Lotus Village (17 Main Street, Stanley, Tel: 2813 1233). They also have cute kids-size outfits. The owners of Lotus Village are very helpful with selection and fittings. Shirts, blouses and suits made of linen material can be found in several stores, and the quality is pretty good. There are a few places selling

Oriental paintings and art pieces, which brightens up the market, but you probably need to know what you are buying before pulling out your wallet. Follow your exploration of the market with a stroll along the waterfront and a visit to the Tin Hau Temple (on Main Street) which is dedicated to the goddess of the sea, before diving into a taxi back to town for a well-earned drink and lunch.

Gough Street (Noho)

Gough Street is a little street not far from Soho (the area known as Noho) and offers a selection of cosy restaurants and cafes, as well as a few creative lifestyle shops. Lunch here followed by a stroll around the shops forms a nice two/three-hour alternative to the buzz of Soho.

Of particular interest in terms of stores is **Ecols** (No 8 & 10 Gough Street, Central, Tel: 3106 4918), which was opened in 2009, and is Hong Kong's first store to sell a range of environmentally friendly lifestyle products. The handbags, wallets, furniture, lamps, vases, jewellery, together with all the materials and lighting that form the shop itself, are eco-friendly. Handbags made of candy wrapper scrap, pull tabs and newspapers are popular and funky. There is a range of recycled teak-wood furniture, by eco designer Dr Singh Intrachooto, which is quite modern and chic in appearance. Moreover, Ecols has become an exhibition space for creatives to share their eco ideas. So, you are likely to see such exhibits during your visit.

Homeless (29 Gough Street, Central, Tel: 2581 1880) is a wonderful store for shopping and browsing contemporary, design-led home and personal stuff. The branch in Gough Street is the flagship. In 2009, it was expanded with a further store opposite. "Homeless" implies that the items in the store are waiting to be taken home, in case you were wondering. Inside is rather like a modern Aladdin's cave with furniture, lighting, home accessories, stationery, personal accessories and various designer items colourfully revealing themselves the further you go inside the store. In fact, the collection of table and over-hanging lamps is impressive. As well as products created by local designers, the store carries over 30 international brands. Even if you don't end up purchasing a lamp or coffee table, you will probably walk out with one of many gadgets (Dead Mark bookmark, Hand sticky notes, Mix Tape USB Stick) dotted around. If you take the stairs outside around the side of the store, you will find Basement, opened by Homeless in 2009 and offering a relaxing and cosy stop point for food and refreshments.

Carrie Chau is one of Hong Kong's top contemporary illustration artists. Her work is based on feelings of happiness and love, and as a result, she has a strong Asian following. **The Wun Ying Gallery** (7 Gough Street, Central, Tel: 2581 1110), part of the Homeless family of stores, is an exhibition space for Chau's work and a store for various Chau-inspired products (T-shirts, notebooks, mugs, tote bags, cushions, card holders, calenders, clocks, etc). If you are looking for an original and slightly quirky gift, which also represents something of contemporary Hong Kong design, this might be just the store. It certainly beats Hello Kitty.

G.O.D

cool!

Hong Kong

G.O.D, which stands for "goods of desire" (although in Cantonese the brand's name sounds like the slang for "to live well"), was founded by local architect Douglas Young in 1997 and has become Hong Kong's benchmark lifestyle store. Items on sale take their lead from the extremes of East and West, new and old, which is a fair reflection of Hong Kong during the 20th century. There are three stores, with the one in Causeway Bay being the brand's flagship and most interesting. Everything that a hip city dweller requires for his/her home, at reasonable prices, can be found in G.O.D—the more popular items being sofas, sheets and pillows, tote bags, chairs, various kitchenware and T-shirts. There is also a fantastic range of art and design books. Bed sheets containing prints of tenement housing and places which have disappeared as a result of modernisation; bags with prints of old-style post boxes; notebook covers with Cantonese movie stars are typical of the other items on sale. Incorporating 20th-century Hong Kong imagery and modelling designs on old colonial Hong Kong (but with a modern twist) is the main thing at G.O.D, which makes for fascinating browsing and the opportunity to find something exotic and Hong Kong-inspired at the same time.

Leighton Centre, Sharp Street East, Causeway Bay
Tel: 2890 5555

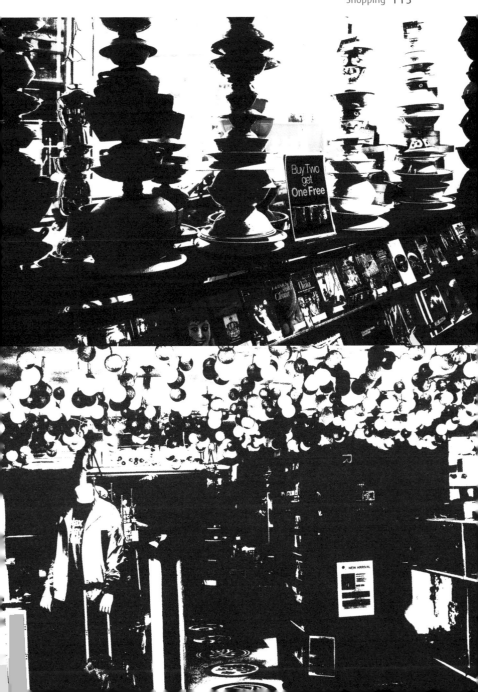

Earth Home

Earth Home is a gem of a shop offering handmade ceramics from Somluk Pantiboon, described as Thailand greatest living ceramicist. Pantiboon lives and works in Chiang Rai in Northern Thailand. Earth Home is the only permanent exhibitor of his work outside of his gallery in Thailand. Working with glazes created from the ash of wood, leaves, rice stalks and bamboo collected from around his home, his ceramics reflect a combination of traditional materials and technique with contemporary expression. Expats, financiers, local celebrities and foreign visitors form Earth Home's main group of clients. Amongst the latter, elegant tea sets, sake cup sets, small pots, bowls and bath ware are especially popular. Earth Home also offers a bespoke service for dinner settings and wash basins. The entrance to the shop is a little tricky to find: it is via the rear laneway between Mee Lun Street and Shin Hing Street. You probably would not expect to find a shop like this in ready-and-go, metropolis Hong Kong, but Earth Home is a wonderful reminder of the subtlety and craft required for the beautiful things in life.

Shop C2, LGF, Po Lung Building, 89-95 Hollywood Road. Central Tel: 2547 0101

Dusty

From relatively humble beginnings in 1997, Dusty has become one of Hong Kong's most successful streetwear brands with an increasing global identity. Dusty has four locations in Hong Kong, with the one in Mongkok being the most recently opened. "Rebel without a pause" is Dusty's slogan and acts as a focal point for the design direction of its high-quality, cutting-edge fashion products. Collaborations with underground artists and other regional brands (Subcrew, NSBQ, Invasian) are a regular occurrence and become collector's items for Dusty's loyal clientele. T-shirts, jeans, shirts, windbreakers, bags and caps are the more popular items. Each new season of fashion is eagerly awaited by customers and the local fashion media. Like its products, the staff at Dusty are cool and give you plenty of space and time to browse.

Shop B, GF, Tak Cheong Commercial Building,
215 Portland Street, Mongkok, Kowloon
Tel: 2789 2177

Beams T

If you are a T-shirt junkie, you should certainly pay a visit to Beams T in Silvercord, a mid-size mall in the heart of Tsim Sha Tsui. Beams T originates from Japan, where it has a following amongst the hip. The Silvercord shop contains one of Beams T's famous T-shirt conveyor belts. The T-shirts themselves are not exactly cheap, but are wonderfully designed and have fashion *cache*. Beams T was brought to Hong Kong by local fashion group I.T. Whilst you are in Silvercord, you should visit some of the other I.T.-owned stores, including X-LARGE, A.P.C. and Montage, Freshjive. Like Beams T, most are from Japan. There's also an I.T. outlet store on the top floor, especially for those who don't fancy trekking all the way out to Ap Lei Chau.

Shop 27, 2F, Silvercord, 30 Canton Road, Tsim Sha Tsui, Kowloon
Tel: 2992 0235

A Bathing Ape

Japanese brand A Bathing Ape (or BAPE) was founded by streetwear marketing pioneer Tomoaki "Nigo" Nagao in 1993 and has become the trendsetter in global hip-hop and urban style fashion. According to Nigo, BAPE is in fact short for "A Bathing Ape in Lukewarm Water". The brand has a huge celebrity following. Their store in Central is relatively new (opened in 2006) and stands glaringly opposite or alongside regal brands such as Joyce, Gucci and Harvey Nichols. In Hong Kong at least, older people like to appear fashionable and contemporary, so there is logic to BAPE's Hong Kong location. In any case, the BAPE store is spectacular and has become a real destination for a mix of people. The sneakers display is very much part of that spectacle. Moreover, the T-shirts, polo shirts, jeans, hats and belts are what the hipsters come for.

G/F, 10 Queen's Road Central, Central
Tel: 2868 9448

I.T.

The I.T. Group has been a true driving force behind the development of modern fashion in Hong Kong. Like many such companies and brands in Hong Kong, I.T.'s origins are humble (a 200-sq.ft. store in 1988) before it grew into the stock-market listed group that it is today, with own-brand stores and other (licensed by I.T.) brand stores in the key retail spots of Hong Kong. The I.T. select stores reflect very well the purpose of the entire group. Carrying a range of just about every A-grade Japanese and Euro label known to fashion man and woman, I.T. wants to make a fashion slave out of you. There are several I.T. select stores around Hong Kong, but the more interesting ones are at Causeway Bay (2 Kingston Street, Tel 2881 6102) and Admiralty (Shop 252, Level 2, Pacific Place, 88 Queensway), making it easy for anyone seeking their dose of shopping for cutting-edge designer fashion. Check out the excellent I.T. website www.ithk.com for details of their other brands and their store locations.

D-mop

D-mop is somewhat the granddaddy of the urban streetwear movement in Hong Kong, having reached its 20th anniversary in 2008. In fact, over the years, D-mop has become a rather diverse select store, offering not just the usual high-end streetwear, but also designer high-fashion (Y-3, Patrick Cox, Miharayauhiro, BLESS) and sports clothing (Nike White Label). There are several D-mop and D-mop Denimstore branches scattered around Hong Kong, with the one on Kingston Street being the flagship (and certainly worth stopping in during your visit to Fashion Walk—see page 88). There is a bias towards wood and construction materials in terms of the interior design, and often, there will be an exhibition of some sort related to the brands D-mop carries. Presentations and displays are highly original and stop shoppers in their tracks. There are probably more cutting-edge stores around, but if you are a little short of time, D-mop is a solid one to visit for its selection and presentation of urban and designer fashion.

Shop A-C, 8 Kingston Street, Causeway Bay
Tel: 2175 4881 Website: www.d-mop.com.hk/

Medium Rare

This concept shop has iconic status amongst streetwear aficionados. It's not so easy to find, but essentially, it is opposite the SOGO building in Causeway Bay. Once inside, there is a tremendous air of calm. Only the small, minority group of ultracool (mainly young) fashionistas seem to enter the doors of Medium Rare. The main draw is largely Japanese streetwear brands which are hard to find—Viridi-anne, Lad Musician, Siva, Sub-ware, Safu—some of which Medium Rare has the exclusive Hong Kong distribution rights to. Also, another draw is the fact that Medium Rare offers the full range of these brands—long and short-sleeve shirts, pants, sweaters, as well as the T-shirts and accessories—unlike other stores which may only have the T-shirts. If you are serious fan of ultrahip street and urban wear, you will probably find something to amaze you at Medium Rare.

1F, 545 Lockhart Road, Causeway Bay
Tel: 2838 3646

Shine

The style conscious, together with local celebrities and models, go to Shine for direction and ideas in forward fashion. Established in 2000, Shine has built a reputation for being Hong Kong's main store for innovative designers from around the world. Shine introduced to Hong Kong premium denim, and continues to be trend central for anyone seeking that one-of-a-kind piece. Besides edgy apparel, the store carries a range of accessories and shoes for men and women. Most likely, you have to be really in the know to recognise some of the brand labels (Ksubi, Corpus, Dictionary, Golem, Gardem Paris, Pelican Avenue, Slow Gun, Guillaume Lemiel). But Shine's ability to select and then fore-front these rising stars makes visiting the store a most refreshing fashion experience.

Cleveland Mansion, 5-7 Cleveland Street, Causeway Bay Tel: 2890 8261

Shanghai Tang

Ask most local Chinese people about Shanghai Tang, and they will
say it's for tourists or expats. Still, the way in which founder and local
entrepreneur David Tang has built Shanghai Tang into a truly global brand
is impressive. And visiting Shanghai Tang's store in the Pedder Building is
a treat and rather like stepping into a Wong Kar-Wai movie with its dark
and opulent colours, and swanky interior. The setting is meant to be
Shanghai during the 1930s. The store assistants wear classical Chinese

cool!

jackets and the cashier cubicles are raised above ground level like in the old days. Fashion wise, this is as good as it gets for Chinese chic. Women's jackets and dresses (*qi paos*) are designed in traditional colours such as neon pink and tart lime. The Mao jackets for men are stylish and have tag names like "Double Fish Tang" and "Velvet Tang". There is a great range of clothing for children. Moreover, Shanghai Tang's flagship carries a wide range of gift items—candles, jewellery boxes, tableware, photo frames, stationery items—each designed with a mix of old and new China. You're a tourist—go to Shanghai Tang!

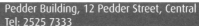

Pedder Building, 12 Pedder Street, Central
Tel: 2525 7333

Kapok

The area around Star Street in Wan Chai is the closest you will get to finding a boho crowd in Hong Kong. And there, opposite a *dai pa dong* (local fast food joint), in St Francis Yard, resides Kapok. Founded by Frenchman Arnault Castell, the lower rents of Wan Chai allows him to showcase and sell whatever pleases his eclectic taste. Hence the distinctive products from Europe and Asia, ranging from CDs to homeware, small furniture, beauty products, stationery (Arnault is the official distributor of Moleskine notebooks in Hong Kong) and books, to jewellery and casual clothing. What bonds them together is Arnault's appreciation for their high standards of craftsmanship and creativity, whether by known or unknown designers and brands. Kapok likes to invite its favourite designers to create products exclusively for the store (for example, a limited edition Moleskine designed by Singapore's h55 Studio), which is highly appreciated by customers. The interior of the store is somewhat like a workshop, with a varnished concrete floor and raw lighting. The staff pretty much leave you to it, but when asked, are knowledgeable about the wide variety of products. Kapok is a tree commonly found in Asia, and certainly this Kapok provides a little shopping oasis in the middle of urban Hong Kong.

5 St Francis Yard, Wan Chai
Tel: 2549 9254

Sin Sin Atelier

Sin Sin is quite an amazing woman who designs widely, from clothes and bags, to jewellery and décor items, not to mention fine art. Her inspiration is strongly Oriental, but at the same time, Sin Sin approaches her work with a Western design mindset. Sin Sin Atelier is the mini-HQ of all of this activity and is located on top of a charming slope near the Cat Street/ Hollywood Road area of Central. On the second floor is Sin Sin's office. Below carries her range of ladies wear, sterling silver jewellery and some very original and cool handbags. Like the owner, the interior is elegant, stylish and charming. If you have a tendency towards simple colours, abstract prints, and brands such as Ann Demulemeester and Issey Miyake, you will certainly appreciate the qualities of this store. Opposite is Sin Sin Annex, an exhibition gallery for mainly South Asian art, and a further reflection of the designer's love of Asian art and culture.

52 Sai Street, Central
Tel: 2521 0308

MADE-TO-MEASURE

You can't beat custom-made clothes, and we all know Hong Kong has plenty of traditional tailors. Usually your hotel concierge can be relied upon to recommend a good tailor, especially if you just want some basic suits, shirts or blouses made up. But you have to look carefully for the more fashion-conscious tailors. The latter are often disguised as just regular boutiques, when in fact they have some of the most creative fashion designers in Hong Kong working behind the scenes. Even for these designers, don't be afraid to bring in clippings from your favourite fashion magazines. They can at least be a starting point. Also, many tailors are happy for you to bring in your own fabrics, but don't expect anything too spectacular out of lesser materials.

At **Fang Fong** (67A Peel Street, Central, Tel: 3105 5557), designer Wu Lai-Fan speaks to her customers to ascertain what they are really looking for. This lengthy consultation then results in sketches of various silhouettes to suit the customer's body shape, from which pieces are designed and created. As a nice extra, Wu advises on accessories to go with the clothes she designs. Wu is a graduate of the Hong Kong Polytechnic University and her work is mainly Asian inspired (*qipao*-collared halter tops made from non-traditional silks, kimono lining dresses). She also customises and alters her customers existing clothes, updating them to the designs of the current season or adding details.

Alex Daye, together with his business partner Ellis Kreuger, are the creators of the menswear label **J.A.Daye** and the women's line **Gertrude Pudding** (2F, Lee Wah Mansion, 171-77 Hollywood Road, Sheung Wan, Tel: 2545 8955). They approach tailoring slightly differently, by starting out with a ready-to-wear collection from which alterations can then be made together with small changes here and there (eg, a different collar). Their approach is classic tailoring with unexpected colours and fabrics to create a certain edge. They also have an online tailoring/ordering service (www.jadaya.com) together with video instructions on how to measure yourself.

Movie star Maggie Cheung had them made here for the movie *In the Mood for Love*; and its telephone number is etched firmly into the address books of every Hong Kong socialite and celebrity. **Linva Tailors** has been making *cheongsams* since the 1960s and tailor Mr Leung has established himself as Hong Kong's *Shifu* (Master) of this traditional Chinese craft which never seems to go completely out of fashion. You can bring your own silk or choose from Master Leung's impressive selection that ranges from basic patterns to special brocades and embroidered silks. You should allow four days from initial fitting to follow-up (remember to bring your heels for both), and then a further two or three weeks for completion. Such craftsmanship can't be rushed. However, delivery to your home can be arranged, including overseas.

Nightlife

THE DAY CERTAINLY DOES NOT COME TO A HALT WHEN THE SUN GOES DOWN. IF ANYTHING, LIFE GETS GOING AS DARKNESS DESCENDS. HONG KONG'S BAR AND CLUB SCENE IS AS GOOD AS IN ANY OTHER MAJOR CITY. AND THERE IS SO MUCH VARIETY. GENERALLY, HONG KONG'S MAIN NIGHT LIFE IS CENTERED IN FOUR AREAS. LAN KWAI FONG IS THE BEST KNOWN OF THEM ALL. YOU GET A MIX OF LOCALS, BUSINESS-TYPES AND TOURISTS ALL GENERALLY HAVING A ROUSING GOOD TIME. NOT FAR IS SOHO, WHICH HAS WONDERFUL BOUTIQUE RESTAURANTS AND PLENTY OF TRENDY BARS. ON THE KOWLOON SIDE, KNUTSFORD TERRACE IN TSIM SHA TSUI HAS TURNED INTO A LIVELY DESTINATION, SIMILAR TO SOHO (MINUS THE ESCALATOR AND THIGH-STRAINING SLOPES). FOR A MORE SLOW-PACED, QUIETER NIGHT OUT, STAR STREET IN WAN CHAI IS AN OPTION TO CONSIDER. IF YOU ARE A VISITOR, TRY TO PERSUADE SOME OF YOUR HIP FRIENDS LIVING IN HONG KONG TO TAKE YOU OUT FOR A NIGHT. IF THAT ISN'T AN OPTION, YOU WON'T GO WRONG BY HITTING ONE OR MORE OF THE PLACES PROFILED HERE.

Dragon-I

Dragon-I is Hong Kong's hottest nightspot. Movie and TV celebrities, pop idols, fashion models, movers and shakers, Premier League footballers—they can all be found at this much-talked-about venue created by local nightclub impresario Gilbert Yeung. So, is there any way mere mortals can enter the Dragon? It's not impossible, if you are friendly enough at the front door and don't look out of place. Inside, there are two main areas. The Red Room is a dining room which becomes the VIP/members area later in the evening. The Playground contains New York-style booth seating, a long bar and a vibrant dance floor. Designed by India Mahdavi, the interior mood is dark and sexy, with red Chinese lanterns enhancing that effect. Mojitos seem to be a big favourite here. And if you are feeling peckish, don't underestimate the Japanese and fusion dishes, which are surprisingly good. Dragon-I has a reputation for bringing in world-class DJs and acts, and putting on unforgettable nights of music and dance. Sure, it's a see-and-be-seen place, but if you are aiming to have a cool time in Hong Kong, you simply have to make a call at Dragon-I.

UGF, 60 Wyndham Street, Central
Tel: 3110 1222 Website: dragon-i.com.hk

1/5 nuevo

Located in the quieter and bohemian area of Star Street, 1/5 nuevo is an altogether more relaxed affair than the bars and clubs found in Soho and Lan Kwai Fong. Opened in 2007, it quickly established itself as a favourite chill-out spot for creative types of all nationalities. These days, following changes to the neighbourhood, financiers and executives are amongst the regulars at this elegant and perfectly formed watering hole. There is a distinctly Mediterranean touch to the design of 1/5 nuevo, which is followed closely by its food and beverage offerings. Sangria, mojito with seasonal fruits, and wine by the carafe are especially popular. For those who fancy a nibble, there is an excellent menu of Mediterranean-inspired finger and bar foods. Actually, if you go beyond the bar area and to the rear, you will find a stylish dining area which serves light but satisfying Mediterranean French and Italian dishes, which has made 1/5 nuevo a popular lunch destination. During the evening, the music is cool, smooth and downtempo, with DJ Edwin performing every Friday and Saturday. For those who are looking for a quieter drink and conversation before heading out to the insanity of LKF and such like, 1/5 nuevo has its advantages. But be warned: you may end up staying all night.

9 Star Street, Wanchai
Tel: 2529 2300 Website: www.elite-concepts.com

Drop

The first challenge is to locate the entrance to this basement club (you would not be the first to end up asking or calling—but essentially, it's not on Hollywood Road, but around the back on the corner of Cochrane Street). The second is getting in if you should arrive after 11 pm during the weekend, when things liven up and it operates a members-only policy (have your concierge to call ahead). When you do finally step in, you do so into a happening place. The space is tight and cosy (120 people), and before 11 pm, you can lounge and chill. After 11 pm, the DJs take over and Drop transforms into the hot party zone that it is famed for. The music is house. On Tuesdays and Saturdays, DJ Joel Lai is on the decks, delivering his unique blend of American-style house. Guest DJs from around the world perform regularly as well, which establishes Drop as Hong Kong's main place for house music. In terms of drinks, Drop's specialty is cocktails, introducing fresh fruit martinis to Hong Kong (try the lychee martini and water melon martini, the two big favourites). Drop has real presence—it's 2,000-odd members are frequent visitors together with major celebs passing through Hong Kong. It also has tradition—Drop was in Soho well before many of the surrounding bars and restaurants turned up.

Basement, On Lok Mansion, 39-43 Hollywood Road, Soho
Tel: 2543 8856   Website: www.drophk.com

Red

One thing that RED has going for it is the fabulous outdoor terrace and breathtaking views of the Central skyline and Victoria Harbour that come with that. Given its location, there is usually a strong contingent of office workers in the evening, but overall, RED provides a very relaxed space to chill out for all concerned. There are tables for large groups of people, as well as places for more intimate occasions away from the hub. The mild sea breeze adds to the occasion. If you can manage to tear yourself away from the great outdoor scene, there is also a vibrant dining and drinking space indoors. Being affiliated to the gym Pure Fitness, RED offers a variety of healthy and light dishes, which might make a nice change from heavy fine dining. Friday and Saturday nights are the big late nights for RED, with live DJs contributing to a sparkling atmosphere until 3 am. The wines, beers, cocktails and selection of foods are all pretty good here. RED's main selling point is the opportunity for *al freso* drinking amongst the skyscrapers of Central, wonderfully friendly bar staff and an environment that is chilled and thankfully unpretentious.

Podium Level 3, 2 IFC, 8 Finance Street, Central
Tel: 8129 8882 Website: www.pure-red.com

Salon de Ning

Sophisticated and ostentatious at the same time, Salon de Ning seems to have made quite an impact since its opening in 2008. Inspired by the private residences of 1930s Shanghai socialite and globetrotter "Madame Ning", this intriguing lounge bar is a fusion of East and West, antique and modern. Designed by Hong Kong-based Henry Leung, there are four themed rooms, each of which has their own fascinating characteristics. L'Afrique Room has a Saharan tent-like setting with walls adorned with tiger skins. The Ski Room resembles a Swiss chalet (with fireplace and very cosy). The Bailar and Boudoir rooms offer glimpses of Madame Ning's personal life and interests. Framed photographs on walls, displays of vintage dresses and hats, jewelry and perfume bottles create an intimate environment. The Ning Sling (Absolut Mandarin, lychee liqueur, passion fruit puree, orange juice and mint leaves) seems the perfect cocktail accompaniment to the glamorous surroundings. During the week, from 9 pm onwards, a live band plays 70s/80s/90s disco music in the main Shanghai art deco lounge area. If that is not quite your thing, go during the weekend, when there is a more ambient beat generated by the DJ on duty.

The Peninsula, B/F, Salisbury Road, Tsim Sha Tsui, Kowloon
Tel: 2315 3188 Website: www.peninsula.com/hongkong

Yumla

There is something very authentic about Yumla. The music comes first; there is no strict door policy; and the people who go there are genuinely more relaxed and fun to be around. Founded by local producer Dan F in 2004, Yumla is located above an urban park, which gives it the added feature of chilled outdoor drinking. The inside space is small, but it soon becomes apparent that this is no deterrent for the many regulars who love the unpretentious, music-driven environment. Resident DJs and international acts offer mainly indie and underground electronica. Indeed, Dan F and Yumla are famed for leading the way for underground club music in Hong Kong. As well as the music, Yumla is heavily into encouraging and backing local creative projects (supporting local artists, funding street magazines, etc). This is why Yumla has become a magnet for creatives, music fans, and alternative celebrities. Even during weekdays, Yumla pulls in the crowds with its extended Happy Hour (until 9 pm). And when things are really happening, it can remain lively until 5 am during weekends.

Lower Basement, 79 Wyndham Street, Central
Tel: 2147 2382   Website: www.yumla.com

Volar

Volar is a key destination for the younger hip and chic crowd of Hong Kong. Officially, it's a members-only club, but out-of-towners can email (intoxicated@volar.com.hk) ahead to get on to the guest list (during weekends, you would also need to pay cover at the door). When he opened Volar in December 2004, owner Ben Ku's main aim was to bring quality electronic music to Hong Kong, and he has succeeded on a pretty big scale. In fact, the music on offer now ranges from hip hop, funky beats, rock, breaks, electro, house to everything in between. Today, fashionistas, celebrities and models mix easily with other stylish, less-known party goers, with music supplied by a roster of leading international DJs which Volar is renowned for bringing in. Volar's cavernous basement occupies over 5,000 sq.ft. and consists of two distinctive spaces. The club area boasts a state-of-the-art sound, lighting and projection system, and is where the music and partying goes on all night. The lounge area, with its gem-studded carousel horses, psychedelic visual arts and ceiling of lush green foliage, creates a slightly surreal environment. The signature drink—Martini Royale (vodka, gin and champagne)—has become a Hong Kong institution. With its underground but chic atmosphere, Volar itself is rapidly becoming a nightlife institution.

Basement, 38-44 D'Aguilar Street, Central
Tel: 2810 1272 Website: www.volar.com.hk

Accommodation

COMPETITION BETWEEN HOTELIERS IN HONG KONG IS INTENSE TO SAY THE LEAST, ESPECIALLY NOW THAT THE NUMBER OF VISITORS HAS INCREASED EXPONENTIALLY FOLLOWING MAINLAND CHINA'S RELAXATION OF TRAVEL TO CAPITALIST HONG KONG FOR MANY OF ITS CITIZENS AND BUSINESSPEOPLE. NEW HOTELS ARE CONSTANTLY SPRINGING UP, EXISTING ONES ARE REGULARLY UPGRADING AND REVAMPING, AS HONG KONG STRIVES TO BECOME THE NUMBER ONE TOURIST AND BUSINESS CENTRE IN ASIA. AS A RESULT, WORLD-CLASS ACCOMMODATION, IN THE FORM OF BOUTIQUE AND QUALITY-BRAND HOTELS, HAS MADE ITS PRESENCE FELT STRONGLY HERE. IN PLANNING YOUR TRIP TO HONG KONG, IT'S REALLY WORTH SPENDING A BIT OF TIME RESEARCHING THE RIGHT HOTEL FOR YOU. THE ONES PROFILED HERE ARE UNIQUE LEADERS IN STYLE, COMFORT AND SERVICE WITHIN THEIR CATEGORY. IF NOTHING ELSE, THEY ACT AS A BENCHMARK FOR YOUR ULTIMATE CHOICE OF ACCOMMODATION IN HONG KONG.

The Luxe Manor

If you are eager to stay on the Kowloon side of Hong Kong, then the only real boutique hotel option is The Luxe Manor. But what an option it is! Enter the lobby and you are confronted by a world inspired by the surrealists (copper and gold mosaic floor, waterfall, crystal lighting), providing a starkly contrasting mood to the outside Kowloon streets. Look carefully, however, and you will find the odd oriental influences reminding you of the hotel's local roots. Many of the art pieces placed throughout the hotel were collected by the owner Marcus Lee on his travels. Humour, quirkiness and stylishness work in tandem in this most designer of boutique hotels. Containing 159 rooms, the standard rooms continue with the surrealist theme but each has their own distinct design characteristics. The six suites on the 12th floor, however, take you further into the realm

Cool!

of fantasy. As soon as you step out of the lift, you are confronted by the richness of the red wallpaper, reminding one of Wong Kar Wai's movie *In the Mood for Love*. Each suite is a world of its own—the Safari Suite is modeled in the form of a tent in Morocco, with starlight shining from the ceiling, and is often the favourite of both hotel staff and guests. The Luxe Manor is also blessed with an excellent Italian restaurant (Aspasia) and very stylish lounge bar (Dada) which has regular clientele for live jazz during Thursday–Sunday. And as part of the overall love for art and the good life, the hotel has an art and wine-tasting appreciation club (Club Miniaci) which is open to guests. Quite simply, this is a hotel experience that you won't find elsewhere in Hong Kong.

39 Kimberley Road, Tsim Sha Tsui, Kowloon
Tel: 3763 8888
Website: www.theluxemanor.com

JIA

Those of you who have stayed at other Philippe Starck-inspired accommodation in New York will be familiar with the teak floors, white-curtained walls and clean lines of JIA, Hong Kong's first ever boutique hotel. Designed by Starck and John Hitchcox, JIA is ultramod in design and has high coolness factor. But its location in the heart of Causeway Bay is also worthy of consideration for those into exploratory shopping. With only 54 rooms, there is a personal and homely feel about the place ("*Jia*" is the Mandarin for "home"). Because most of the hotel space is not open to the public, there is also a nice atmosphere of intimacy, with staff knowing the names of each of its guests fairly soon after you check in. The rooms range from 380 sq.ft. to suites measuring 780 sq.ft., (as well as the 1,570 sq.ft. penthouse), with each containing a kitchenette and various high-tech gadgetry. White is the dominant colour in all the rooms, which provides a calming and sensuous contrast to the mesh of colours outside in Causeway Bay. To get you started, a healthy complimentary continental breakfast is served in the lobby area, as well as afternoon cakes and evening wine later on. JIA offers its guests further nice touches: access to KEE private members' club, use of the nearby gym, a wide-ranging and flexible room service menu and, if you are inclined, complimentary self-laundry facilities. Refined and intimate, JIA offers the classic boutique hotel experience.

1-5 Irving Street, Causeway Bay
Tel: 3196 9000 Website: www.jiahongkong.com

Langham **Place**

No one would be too surprised if your first impression of Langham Place was one of an art gallery masquerading as a hotel. Indeed, *Time Asia* magazine selected it as such in 2005. With over 1,500 mainly contemporary pieces of Chinese art (ranging from local artists such as Alanala Lau and Hu Yong Yi to more famous Chinese artists like Yue Min Jun and Qin Da Hu), the hotel even offers its guests guided art tours. The Red Guard, Good Morning and Tsing Ma Bridge art pieces are particularly worth stopping by at. The art-centric nature of the hotel extends even to the design of in-room literature. Opened in 2004, with 665 rooms over 42 floors, Langham Place is large and tall, but has the sophistication, atmosphere and high-tech wizardry of a modern boutique hotel. Standard rooms are 350 sq.ft., are suitable for any gadget-loving guest (docking home for i-pod, flat-screen TV, DVD/CD player, Cisco IP phone system), and have floor-to-ceiling windows which (if you get the right room) offers fascinating views of the streets of Mongkok. Rather than distance itself, the hotel embraces its

neighbourhood, offering guests tours of the nearby Mongkok market and streets—a sampling of the real Kowloon. The hotel also has an impressive environmental policy. Under environmental manager Jor Fan, many products used by Langham Place are either recyclable or degradable. The Ming Court Chinese restaurant within the hotel is Michelin-starred (see page 46) and the Chuan Spa offers guests sophisticated spa, fitness and swimming pool facilities. For travellers with children, Langham Place is an excellent option for its amenities and flexible staff. In general, this hotel is a hidden gem in the high-octane streets of Tsim Sha Tsui.

555 Shanghai Street, Mongkok, Kowloon
Tel: 3552 3388 Website: www.langhamhotels.com

Four Seasons

If it is space and style that you are looking for, the Four Seasons offers standard rooms measuring 484 sq.ft. that are packed with features to ensure you have a comfortable (bordering on unforgettable) stay. You can choose between two styles of room: traditional Chinese décor (albeit a contemporary take on it) or Western-style design. 70% of the rooms face Hong Kong Harbour and the remaining 30% face the Peak. Wall-to-wall windows provide captivating views of both. And as in most Four Seasons hotels, the bathroom is luxurious. If you need to do some work or require a further dose of luxury and style, try the Executive Club Lounge on the 45th floor, which offers an array of complimentary amenities and services. Non-executive guests can gain access for a fee. Located in the IFC (International Finance Centre), the hotel sees a mix of business and leisure travellers. For the latter, the IFC Mall (see page 81) offers serious shopping and the Four Seasons has its own direct lift to the Lane Crawford department store there. The restaurant scene at the Four Seasons is vibrant and contains two of the finest within their cuisine category: the Michelin two-star Caprice (French) (see page 50) and the Michelin three-star Lung King Heen (Cantonese) (see page 52). The Blue Bar, famous for its choice of 88 blue cocktails, offers guests a lively and chic late-night venue. Situated on floors 5–7 is the hotel's legendary spa (see page 12) and two infinity pools that not only provides you with views of the Harbour but also music underwater to leave no stone unturned in your pampering. Staying here will require a healthy credit card, but it's hard to ignore the Four Seasons for the experience it offers.

8 Finance Street, Central
Tel: 3196 8888 Website: www.fourseasons.com/hongkong

Located more or less in the heart of Hong Kong's buzzing Lan Kwai Fong area, Hotel LKF is a very stylish boutique hotel that serves as a gradual transition from the party scene outside to an altogether calmer environment. Opened in 2006, it has already picked up several awards (*Business Traveller* magazine's "Best Boutique Hotel in Asia Pacific 2009"), including in the interior design category (by top local design firm Cream Design). As soon as you walk into the lobby, one gets an immediate sense of intimacy and comfort. Standard rooms are 500 sq.ft and are generous

in furnishings (Aeron chair), appliances (42-inch flatscreen, i-pod docking station, Illy expresso machine) and little luxuries (Molten Brown bathroom products, proper fluffy slippers). Each room is different in terms of layout, lighting configuration and wall decoration. Rooms 02 and 08 are deemed favourites by the staff for the rain showers and Room 08 for the view over HK Government Garden. And like all good boutique hotels, the staff has the uncanny ability to address you by your name when they bump into you during your stay. With 95 rooms, Hotel LKF seems just the right size and has become a favourite with many (40% of guests return). Moreover, located on the 29/30th floors is Azure, a contemporary restaurant (A *Hong Kong Tatler* Best Restaurant 2008-09—see page 54) and lounge bar (with pool table) that fits in effortlessly with the rest of the hotel's intimate and cool ambiance. Selected by the *Sunday Times* as one of the world's top 10 sky bars, the outdoor terrace at Azure is worth stepping out on. In short, there's a lot going for Hotel LKF, and you certainly won't have far to stagger back after a night out in Lan Kwai Fong.

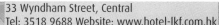

33 Wyndham Street, Central
Tel: 3518 9688 Website: www.hotel-lkf.com.hk

The Landmark

Located in the heart of Central, the Landmark Mandarin Oriental has become the hotel of choice for visiting glitterati and fashionistas. This luxury boutique hotel boasts 113 of Hong Kong's largest rooms, designed by Peter Remedios, each containing a high mix of modern elegance and cutting-edge technology. The stunning glass-walled bathrooms take up one-third of the total room area, which simply adds to the overall feeling of spaciousness and tranquility. There are no views to speak of in any of the rooms, but that seems adequately compensated for by the

sophisticated design and facilities. The MO Bar, designed by Adam Tihany, is most definitely one of the hip meeting places in this part of town. During the morning and day, there is a vibrant breakfast-lunch (the cheeseburger is almost legendary)-afternoon tea crowd. But as the night descends, and the cocktails take over, it becomes increasingly lively and less predictable. On the occasional evenings, you might find artists performing unplugged sessions (as Alicia Keys and John Legend have done in the recent past). The hotel also contains the Amber (see page 56), one of the finest French restaurants in Hong Kong, with extraordinary interior design also by Adam Tihany. And if that is not enough, there is the Oriental Spa (see page 6) which features extremely popular pilates and yoga studios/classes. The Landmark Mandarin Oriental offers an amazing package in terms of luxury, style and hipness. Used to dealing with creative and celeb types, even the concierge staff can be relied on to provide recommendations and make arrangements for a truly cool time in Hong Kong.

15 Queen's Road, Central
Tel: 2132 0188 Website: www.mandarinoriental.com

cool!

W Hong Kong

Located in the up and coming West Kowloon area is W Hong Kong. Opened in 2008, W's typical chic urban style fits effortlessly into the Hong Kong landscape, and is rapidly becoming one of the territory's social hot spots. Staying at the W is as much about entertainment and indulgence as it is about room comfort. All W hotels seem able to deliver a remarkably hip and relaxed environment and W Hong Kong does not disappoint. The Living Room lounge symbolises much of what is right about W Hong Kong. Casual but sexy and chic at the same time, there is often something interesting and edgy going on in the evenings. As for its restaurants, Fire offers hearty, contemporary cuisine (excellent lamb, steak and seafood dishes) in an appropriately red modern setting created by leading Japanese designer Yasimuchi Morita. Kitchen is a modern bistro which is gaining a reputation for being one of Hong Kong's more interesting dining options (see page 59). On the food and beverage side, W Hong Kong has swiftly established itself as being on the edge. The rooms are nothing less than a sanctuary from the buzz and neon of city life outside. Room design is infused with the elements of wood, fire, earth, water and metal, but manages to retain a great sense of minimalism and space. The standard (Wonderful) rooms are 400 sq. ft and have all the amenities that you would expect from any luxury hotel. Ask for a room facing the Western Harbour for terrific views as you lie back on the chaise lounge. To round things off, and for further indulgence, W Hong Kong boasts Bliss (see page 10), which was selected as Hong Kong's best spa of 2008 (*Time Out* Hong Kong).

1 Austin Road West, Kowloon Station, Kowloon
Tel: 3717 2222 Website: www.whotels.com/hongkong

Escapes

IF YOU NEED TO TAKE A MOMENTARY BREAK FROM THE FRENETIC BEAST THAT IS HONG KONG, ART AND CULTURE OFFERS AN ESCAPE FOR MIND AND BODY. FOLLOWING ITS HANDOVER TO CHINA IN 1997 IN PARTICULAR, HONG KONG INVESTED GENEROUSLY IN ITS MUSEUMS OF CULTURE AND HISTORY, PROVIDING LOCALS AND VISITORS WITH A DEEPER APPRECIATION OF HOW HONG KONG CAME TO BE WHAT IT IS TODAY. BUT PERHAPS UNDERRATED IS THE SIMPLICITY OF TAKING A WALK IN SOME OF THE OLDER PARTS OF HONG KONG WHICH OFFERS VISITORS MOMENTS OF STILLNESS AND NEW DISCOVERY. IN TERMS OF CONTEMPORARY ARTS, THE SCENE IN HONG KONG HAS NEVER BEEN MORE RICH AND DIVERSE, CULMINATING IN TWO MAJOR ANNUAL EVENTS ON THE CULTURAL CALENDAR: THE CITY FESTIVAL AND THE HONG KONG INTERNATIONAL FILM FESTIVAL. AND IF YOU WANT ESCAPISM OF THE OPPOSITE EXTREME, WELL, THERE'S ALWAYS THE GLITZ OF MACAU, THE CASINO MECCA OF ASIA.

Dr Sun Yat-Sen Museum

Regarded as the founding father of the Republic of China, Sun Yat-Sen came to Hong Kong for his secondary education and then went on to attend The College of Medicine for Chinese there. During this significant period of his life, Dr Sun decided to engage in and lead revolutionary activity which ultimately led to the overthrow of the Qing Dynasty (and autocracy) in 1911 and the establishment of the Republic of China. The Dr Sun Yat-Sen Museum is a fascinating memorial to this important figure in modern Chinese history. There are two permanent exhibitions. The "Dr Sun Yat-Sen and Modern China" exhibition tells the story of Dr Sun's transformation from student to revolutionary leader. The "Hong Kong in Dr Sun Yat-Sen's Time" offers a fascinating glimpse of the political, economic and social conditions of Hong Kong during the early 1900s prior to the new China forming. The museum is housed in the Kom Tong Hall which was built in 1914 as a private residence and features a mix of Western and Chinese architectural designs. If you can avoid the parties of school kids, this is an engaging museum of history, in an elegant setting, to while away an hour in.

7 Castle Road, Mid-Levels, Central
Tel: 2367 6573
Website: www.lcsd.gov.hk/ce/museum/sysm

Museum of Art

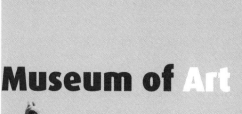

One of the most impressive collections of Chinese art in the world is contained in the Hong Kong Museum of Art. There are seven exhibition galleries that display Chinese antiquities, Chinese fine arts, historical pictures and contemporary Hong Kong art. In all, there are some 15,000 objects of art, providing a cultural record of decoration and objects designed for both daily use and ritualistic purposes. A must-see is the famous Xubaizhai collection of Chinese paintings and calligraphy which dates from the Northern Dynasties (386–581) through to the modern day. The contemporary gallery presents a mix of traditional Chinese and Western techniques, reflecting Hong Kong's modernisation and its unique exposure to the West. Besides the permanent exhibitions, there are regular special displays of international art collections which are very popular with local art lovers. The museum's design and lay out affords plenty of space in between exhibits, enabling visitors to marvel comfortably at these fascinating artefacts and pieces of art. If there is one museum that you should visit whilst here, which gives you a greater understanding of Hong Kong from a cultural and historical perspective, the Hong Kong Museum of Art is probably the one.

10 Salisbury Road, Tsim Sha Tsui, Kowloon
Tel: 2721 0116 Website: www.lcsd.gov.hk/ce/museum/arts

Fringe Club

For more adventurous and contemporary performances and exhibitions, try the Hong Kong Fringe Club in Central. There is a regular and diverse programme of performances, including live rock, alternative and jazz music (mainly starting at 10.30 pm), which can be booked in advance. The Fringe Club provides rent-free facilities for local and overseas artists and performers. It has become the hub of contemporary art in Hong Kong and organises the annual City Festival (similar to the Edinburgh Fringe Festival). The red-and-white striped building itself was built in the 1890s in Edwardian style. In 1982, the Fringe Club took up space in the south section, with the Foreign Correspondents Club occupying the north. During the evenings, the Fringe Club's roof garden becomes a popular haunt for intellectuals, artists and bohemian types.

2 Lower Albert Road, Central
Tel: 2521 7251 Website: www.hkfringeclub.com.hk

If you really feel the urge to get properly out of the city centre and onto the water, you can of course head for the outlying islands, such as Lantau (the largest, but with Hong Kong Disneyland now adding an extra dimension), Lamma (authentic old Hong Kong thanks to the ban on motor vehicles) and Sai Kung (charming fishing villages and seafront restaurants). But for a surreal island experience, go for Macau. This 10-square-mile dot generates more gambling revenue than Las Vegas and Atlantic City combined. The recent arrival of a new kid in the form of American casino entrepreneur Sheldon Adelson and his $12 billion Vegas-style strip, complete with a replica of Venice and its canals and singing gondoliers, as well as spanking new shopping malls, has transformed at least one part of Macau. The other part of this island is rather more charismatic and sleepy. This is the old Macau—the fortresses, cobbled back streets, churches and food—under the influence of its former Portuguese

colonial masters. This unique fusion of East and West was recognised by UNESCO when, in 2005, it designated 30 buildings and squares collectively as the Historic Centre of Macau World Heritage Site. Due to its further modernisation, Macau these days has a number of excellent fine-dining options in and around the casinos and up-scale hotels. But why not try out some of the proven local Portuguese establishments. Often no-frills, they nevertheless offer outstanding dishes. Two of the island's favourites are Antonio Restaurante (Rua dos Negociantes No. 3, Taipa, Tel: 2899 9998) and Restaurante Fernando (9 Hac Sa Beach, Coloane, Tel: 2888 2264). For both, it is probably best to book ahead. If you are feeling peckish still later, stop at Lord Stow Bakery (1 Rua do Tsassara, Coloanne, Tel: 2888 2534) for a famous egg tart. End the evening with drinks at glamorous 38, atop the Crown Macau, which has great indoor and outdoor views (38F, Crown Macau, Avenue de Kwong Tung, Taipa, Tel: 2886 8888). To get to Macau from Hong Kong, there are round-the-clock turbojets (www.turbojet.com.hk, Tel: 2921 6688) that take approximately one hour. You can probably make your visit to Macau in one day. But during the weekends, enthusiastic gamblers sail in on Saturday, gamble the night away, before returning Sunday morning in time for *dim sum*.

Hollywood Road

Hollywood Road can easily provide a satisfying morning's worth of walking and browsing for anyone interested in works of art, antiques and curios. Hilly, winding and quaint, it is a street of discovery and seemingly undisturbed by time. Mid-morning does seem the best time to take in Hollywood Road (except Sundays, when most of the shops are shut). Start in Hollywood Road Park (in Sheung Wan), where you will find photographs showing the history of the area. At the intersection with Po Yan Street, you will come across Cat Street Gallery (No.222), an airy, large space dedicated to contemporary art by emerging as well as established artists. Opposite, on Po Yan Street, is Para/Site, an edgy exhibition space for installations by local artists. Nextdoor is the Lomography store, which stocks Lomo cameras, films and accessories, together with various exhibits of this analog form of photography. Continuing along Hollywood Road, heading west, at No.222 is the Asia Art Archive (on the 7th floor), which is the only archive in the world focusing on contemporary Asian art. If you are not careful, you can blow your entire morning here. In the same building, in the basement level, is Tang Contemporary, which has exhibited significant names in contemporary Asian art.

Moving along, down Upper Lascar Row (also known as Cat Street Bazaar), is where things get a little more touristy. A mix of antique shops and open-air curio market stalls, everything from Mao badges and caps, snuff bottles and old postcards to Ming dynasty furniture, paintings and lotus lamps can be found here. This is the zone for bargain hunters and those seeking eclectic souvenirs. Once you have battled your way through to the end of Upper Lascar Row, turn right up Ladder Street, back onto Hollywood Road, and cross for Man Mo Temple. Built in 1848, it honours (perhaps strangely) both the God of Literature and the God of War. Go inside to get a face full of heavy incense smoke and see the colourful statues of these two Gods. Fortune telling is also on offer here.

$5

The Classified Deli and Press Room Bistro (No.108) offers light refreshments or lunch mainly of the European kind. From here onwards you will encounter a host of established antique shops and galleries. Chak's (No.76) and Lam & Co (No.44) specialise in ancient ceramics and porcelains, together with stories to tell about each major piece. Contemporary by Angela Li (Nos.90-92), Cais Gallery (No.54) and Plum Blossoms (No.1) represent contemporary Asian artists. In between these are other galleries and shops showcasing everything from ancient terracotta to lacquered furniture, not to mention the various side roads and alleys off Hollywood Road with their own delights (check out Elgin Street and Old Bailey Street if you have time).

Q&A WITH HONG KONG INSIDERS

MICHAEL LOGAN WORKS AT THE *SOUTH CHINA MORNING POST*, WHERE HE IS THE NEWSPAPER'S MULTIMEDIA EDITOR.

Q: What do you like most about Hong Kong?

Michael: I like Hong Kong's energy and entrepreneurial spirit. There's an old Chinese saying: "It's better to be the head of a chicken than the tail of a donkey." That's definitely true here. People want to work for themselves and they're not afraid to undertake new endeavours.

Q: Where do you like to go in Hong Kong to chill out?

Michael: I find the cinema to be the most relaxing place in Hong Kong. While Hong Kong's offering for independent films is rather weak, the local film industry produces some great stories that are easily missed overseas. I usually take in local films at the President Theatre in Causeway Bay.

Q: What are your favourite restaurants for (i) relaxed/easy dining and (ii) for more special occasions?

Michael: I'm a big steak eater but can't afford to eat at Morton's every week. For something easier on the pocket (but still quite tasty), the recently opened Italian steakhouse Bistecca does the trick for me. For entertaining out-of-town guests, a trip to Yung Kee is pretty much mandatory.

Q: What are your favourite bars or clubs in Hong Kong?

Michael: I have no real favourite bars or clubs. But for a relaxed gathering among friends, Club 71 is the perfect meeting spot.

Q: Where do you like to shop for your wardrobe?

Michael: I usually stick to the "high street" stores in Times Square or IFC. If you need a tailor, I would recommend Jantzen Tailor. For inexpensive casual clothes, there are a few boutiques in Oriental 188 Shopping Centre that I favour.

Q: What are the biggest changes to Hong Kong you have seen over the past five years (or however long you have been in Hong Kong)?

Michael: Hong Kong is pretty consistent in that change is always happening. Bars, restaurants and stores are here one day and then gone the next. But the energy and entrepreneurial spirit here—even in bad times—that never changes.

Q: Are there any hidden gems or less known destinations in Hong Kong that you could recommend?

Michael: Hong Kong has a reputation for gadget shopping. If you're in the market for a camera, I would stay away from the shops in TST. Unless you know what you're doing, you'll be overcharged. Almost any device, computer, phone, etc you need can be found at either Broadway or Fortress. But for speciality gadgets, I tend to visit 298 Computer Zone in Wanchai and for gaming the Oriental 188 Shopping Centre in Wanchai. Another must-visit is the Golden Computer Arcade and the market on Apliu Street in Sham Shui Po.

MAGGIE LEUNG IS A PUBLIC RELATIONS PRACTITIONER IN HONG KONG.

Q: What do you like most about Hong Kong?

Maggie: Everything is so nearby as such that you can just go to a convenient store or 24-hour supermarket and get whatever you want even at midnight! Moreover, Hong Kong is always so energetic; people here are optimistic and tough which helps Hong Kong to survive from many crises like the IT bubbles back in the 90s, SARS and the economic crisis of 2009. I also love the blend of heritage and modernity because there are a lot of historical buildings/sites to explore in Hong Kong while at the same time seeing all the skyscrapers and hi-tech developments spring up.

Q: Where do you like to go in HK to chill out?

Maggie: I prefer small group gatherings with a few close friends, so those private dining places are always my favourite. I also like to organise dinners at my place and invite some friends over so we can all chill and chit-chat (and gossip!).

Q: What are your favourite restaurants for (i) relaxed/easy dining and (ii) for more special occasions?

Maggie: I strongly suggest those private dining places (for instance, I always go to one called Chez Moi, French, and another called Zone-D, Italian, both in Causeway Bay) which really allows you to enjoy a relaxed/cozy dinner. For special occasions, I actually prefer to stay home and cook some simple food.

Q: What are your favourite bars or clubs in HK?

Maggie: For happy hour or chit-chat with friends, I like Zentro in IFC as the atmosphere is easy and friendly. I am not really a clubbing person now so I don't really have a particular one in mind.

Q: Where do you like to shop for your wardrobe?

Maggie: I like to explore different areas to look for special items—so really, everywhere. One thing though is I always look for quality and not just the brand.

Q: What are the biggest changes to HK you have seen over the past five years (or however long you have been in HK)?

Maggie: I would say the people in Hong Kong have definitely become more health-conscious and cautious, which is good! But what I hate is the problem of pollution which is getting increasingly worst. Hong Kong is really my home and I don't want to see it "dying".

7. Are there any hidden-gems or less-known destinations in HK that you could recommend?

Maggie: Go to all the islands! Tung-Lung island is always my first choice; the landscape is just perfect for photography!

FASHION WALK 名店坊

Q: What do you like most about Hong Kong?

Liz: I love the fact that you can go hiking, go to the beach and still have a posh dinner or an urban experience all on the same day. I also think the Hong Kong skyline is one of the most stunning and distinctive in the whole world. The melange of the modern skyscrapers and the charming old colonial/retro buildings is very unique.

Q: Where do you like to go in HK to chill out?

Liz: South Bay Beach is one of the best places for weekend sundowners—they have DJs spinning sunset sessions on weekends and is Hong Kong's answer to Mykonos. Shek-O beach is really groovy and the town is really cute. There are two great spots there—a bar called Paradiso and a restaurant called Black Sheep Cafe. Both those businesses embody the quirkiness of the little village.

Q: What are your favourite restaurants for (i) relaxed/easy dining and (ii) for more special occasions?

Liz: I'm a big fan of Sahara on lower Elgin and La Kasbah on Arbuthnot Road for a convivial, exotic atmosphere. I love the Brunch Club on Peel Street when I'm feeling pensive and want to relax with a book. The Pawn has an amazing colonial atmosphere. The Aqua Group restaurants like Hutong and Yun Fu have mysterious Chinese decor and are great for a special occasion.

Q: What are your favourite bars or clubs in HK?

Liz: Sevva—unbeatable terrace and an upscale crowd of successful people. Go for happy hour on weekends when they have a live DJ and Saxophonist.
Dragon-I—the spot for model and celeb spotting. The entertainment line-up (DJs, dancers and live performances) is always really good.
Lei Doh—romantic bar with quirky European décor. It's a great place to chill with friends or take a date.
Yumla—a fun alternative crowd with an amazing sound system. The owners are true music lovers and they usually have great DJs.
Solas—a Wyndham street staple. This place is super popular with expats. They are always throwing great events there.

Q: Where do you like to shop for your wardrobe?

Liz: In Causeway Bay, around Fashion Walk, Times Square and all the surrounding lanes and alleys which have cool treasures to unearth.

Q: What are the biggest changes to HK you have seen over the past five years (or however long you have been in HK)?

Liz: Seeing Soho being developed and the property market go through a roller coaster ride. The local people have become more considerate, polite and more aware of green issues like cleaning the air and recycling.

Q: Are there any hidden-gems or less-known destinations in HK that you could recommend?

Liz: Millionare's Bay in Sai Kung which is only accesible by private yacht or junk boat. Hire Jaspas Junk to go there. Full Cup Cafe in Mongkok is an artists enclave that few people know about. They built a brand new retro floor and have a cool urban terrace. Sham Shui Po and Lai Chi Kok have great shopping for fashionistas and creative types that like to make their own clothes and accessories. Sham Shui Po also has a really interesting snake restaurant at exit A1 and a street flea market that sells all kinds of campy vintage knick-knacks.

DAN F IS A MUSIC PRODUCER AND THE FOUNDER OF THE SOHO NIGHT CLUB YUMLA.

Q: What do you like most about Hong Kong?

Dan: Travelling around SE Asia is easy from Hong Kong, due to it's location. Also the air pollution blowing in from mainland China 10 months per year is fantastic; the way it catches the evening sunlight and turns everything curry-paste yellow is so picturesque. Where else in the civilised world do you still get to see these things?!

Q: Where do you like to go in HK to chill out?

Dan: To be honest, if I'm not partying at Yumla, then I'm chilling out with friends at my recording studio (which has a terrace, big kitchen and BBQ). Having friends over for dinner and drinks really doesn't get any better and you can *really* relax...something that's usually impossible in any of the commercial restaurants. Fact of Hong Kong—if a food place is good—then it's usually packed.

Q: What are your favourite restaurants for (i) relaxed/easy dining and (ii) for more special occasions?

Dan: It's all about Tsui Wah! Their Malay-style fish curry has been one of the staples in my diet. Otherwise places like The Press Room are good for Western food and cheese. Also I need to mention the Nepalese Social Club in Wan Chai: they make the best fried chili pork and momo in Hong Kong.

Q: What are your favourite bars or clubs in HK (besides Yumla)?

Dan: There aren't any. I am a fascist when it comes to music and Yumla was built to prevent me from going completely insane. If you actually like MTV hip-hop, cover bands or crappy commercial dance music then knock yourself out in Lan Kwai Fong...spoilt for choice.

Q: Where do you like to shop for your wardrobe?

Dan: Online or tailor made. I'm over 6 feet tall and not exactly skinny, so forget trying to buy anything locally! A quick note, many of the tailors here will send your measurements over the border to be machine made. If you want something decent quality, hand-made and traditionally assembled (not to mention perfectly cut) then check out Yeun's Tailor in Central.

Q: What are the biggest changes to HK you have seen over the past five years (or however long you have been in HK)?

Dan: I've been here 10 years. Major changes include the government getting more ineffectual at doing what's best for the citizens—I keep hearing the phrase "inhongkongpetant" which sums up the administration perfectly—and the developers and civil construction companies being allowed to basically wreck the city and harbour front without any thought for the environment or future. Also the gap between rich and poor is growing at a frightening rate, but then this is the same throughout all PRC, not just Hong Kong.

Q: Are there any hidden-gems or less-known destinations in HK that you could recommend?

Dan: Cheung Sha beach on Lantau. It's not exactly hidden but the fact that residents here are exceptionally lazy means that the 40-minute trip (from Central) prevents this beach from ever getting busy. On a sunny day Cheung Sha is unbelievably beautiful. If some remote island beach in Thailand had an international shipping lane two miles offshore, then that would be Cheung Sha.

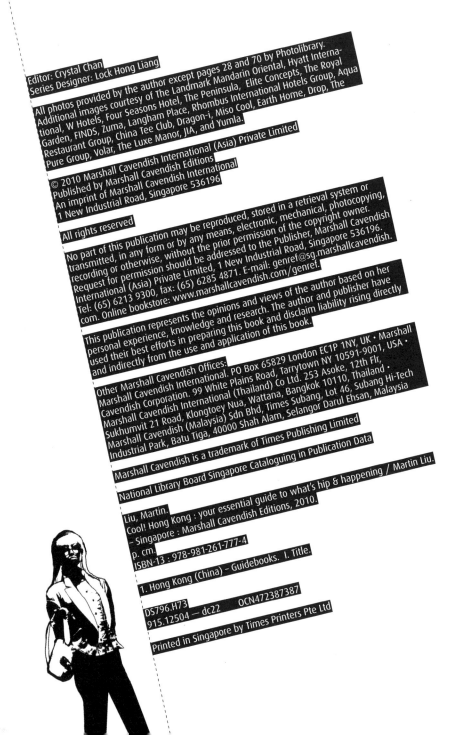

Editor: Crystal Chan
Series Designer: Lock Hong Liang

All photos provided by the author except pages 28 and 70 by Photolibrary.
Additional images courtesy of The Landmark Mandarin Oriental, Hyatt Interna-
tional, W Hotels, Four Seasons Hotel, The Peninsula, Elite Concepts, The Royal
Garden, FINDS, Zuma, Langham Place, Rhombus International Hotels Group, Aqua
Restaurant Group, China Tee Club, Dragon-i, Miso Cool, Earth Home, Drop, The
Pure Group, Volar, The Luxe Manor, JIA, and Yumla.

National Library Board Singapore Cataloguing in Publication Data

Liu, Martin.
Cool! Hong Kong : your essential guide to what's hip & happening / Martin Liu.
– Singapore : Marshall Cavendish Editions, 2010.
p. cm.
ISBN-13 : 978-981-261-777-4

1. Hong Kong (China) – Guidebooks. I. Title.

DS796.H73   OCN472387387
915.12504 — dc22

Printed in Singapore by Times Printers Pte Ltd